PANDEMIC POWER

CEU PRESS PERSPECTIVES

How did we get to the precarious state that we find ourselves in today? What new thinking is needed to tackle the big problems we face? Offering the latest perspectives on both new and perennial issues, books in this series address a wide range of topics of critical importance. An international collection of leading authors encourages us to look at topics from different viewpoints; to think outside the box. Launched to commemorate 30 years of the CEU Press, the series looks to stimulate debates on the broader issues of the day.

Published in the series:

» Matt Qvortrup, *The Political Brain: The Emergence of Neuropolitics*
» Per Högselius and Achim Klüppelberg, *The Soviet Nuclear Archipelago: A Historical Geography of Atomic-Powered Communism*
» Éric Fassin, *State Anti-Intellectualism and the Politics of Gender and Race*

Forthcoming in the series:

» Ranabir Samaddar, *Biopolitics from Below: Crisis, Conjuncture, Rupture*

PANDEMIC POWER

The Covid Response and the Erosion of Democracy

A Liberal Critique

Muriel Blaive

CEU PRESS

Central European University Press
Budapest–Vienna–New York

Published in 2025 by
Central European University Press

Nádor utca 11, H-1051 Budapest, Hungary
E-mail: ceupress@press.ceu.edu
Website: https://www.aup.nl/en/imprint/ceu-press

Research funded by the Austrian Science Fund (FWF) via Elise Richter grant no. V912-G. Published with the support of the Austrian Science Fund (FWF): PUB 1183-P (DOI: 10.55776/PUB1183.)

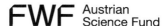

FWF Austrian Science Fund

ISBN 978-963-386-933-8 (paperback)
ISBN 978-963-386-934-5 (ebook)
ISSN 3004-1430

Library of Congress Cataloging-in-Publication Data is available

"*Pandemic Power* is a decisive intervention in the growing critical literature from the social sciences and humanities on the Covid-19 pandemic response. Muriel Blaive draws brilliantly on her expertise as a historian of communism to ask searching questions both about the pandemic and of the response of the liberal left to it. Her argument is compelling: without a full engagement with its missteps during the pandemic, the academic and political left cannot overcome the divisions and authoritarian impulses of the new Trump era."

Toby Green, King's College London

"Much more than a book about Covid, this is a plea for the possibility of critical debate—essential to both science and democracy. Muriel Blaive brilliantly highlights the responsibility of (social) scientists and politicians who, by accepting the rules of the neoliberal game, have abandoned the defense of freedom of expression and the rights of the most vulnerable—traditional left-wing causes—leaving them to the far-right."

Éloïse Adde, Central European University

"There is certainly no shortage of books analyzing responses to the Covid pandemic, many of which have monopolized scholarly attention in recent years, often with an apocalyptic flair. Yet most follow a predictable pattern: they either extol policies such as lockdowns and mandatory vaccinations, critique their impact on minorities and women while studiously avoiding any fundamental questioning of their compatibility with liberal democracy, or, conversely, veer into conspiracy theories and outright Covid denialism.

Muriel Blaive's book stands out precisely because it does none of these. With encyclopedic erudition, razor-sharp logic, and eloquent prose, Blaive methodically dismantles the notion that locking down populations and imposing mandatory vaccinations with fines could ever be reconciled with liberal democracy and the rule of law. More strikingly, she demonstrates that such measures were indefensible even as emergency exceptions, given the statistical evidence available just months after the outbreak.

As the author brilliantly exposes, the mainstream approach to pandemic governance in Western democracies was shaped by extreme censorship and a betrayal by the left of poorer social classes—who, unlike their laptop-class counterparts, lacked the privilege of working remotely. Particularly sharp is her critique of the role played by the media, politicians, and academics in perpetuating these policies and fueling mass hysteria, often with a level of hypochondriac rhetoric that would have made even the most anxious Victorian physician blush."

Uladzislau Belavusau, University of Amsterdam

"This marvelous short book offers a comprehensive and thought-provoking discussion of "Covid censorship," initiated by democratic governments and endorsed by liberal intellectuals to silence dissenting voices challenging the dominant expert narrative. *Pandemic Power* is a lucid analysis of contemporary surveillance democracies, which tend to abandon their core values and commitments—such as freedom of expression—in times of crisis."

András Bozóki, Central European University

Contents

Figures

Acknowledgements

Thank you from the bottom of my heart to the friends who quietly supported my efforts to question the official Covid narrative at a time when it felt somewhat subversive to do so, especially Hynek Pallas, José Faraldo, James Kapaló, Uladzislau Belavusau, Jean-Pierre Ostertag, Claudia Graband, Milan Hanyš, Agnès Lesage, Lukáš Kraus, Annina Gagyiová, Paddington Tucker, Michel Teboul, Jean-Paul Teboul, Lola Gruber, Marián Lóži, Gérard-Daniel Cohen, Estelle Calvy, Jitka Pallas, and Jiří Pallas. You all have kept me sane, and I am tremendously grateful for your encouragements.

Special thanks to my father, Bruno Blaive, who refreshed my memory about his career as professor of medicine and hospital department head, as well as to my godfather, Henri Nussbaumer, for his encouraging comments on the first draft of this book. I am also deeply grateful to the peer reviewers for providing me with insightful comments and references. Thank you as well to D. Alan Dean, Anthony Mckeown, Warren Pearce, Jenin Younes, Mario Gollwitzer, and Christopher Elliott, who generously shared with me the information or references I needed.

Heartfelt thanks to Jen McCall, Linda Kunos, and especially Tony Mason at CEU Press, who encouraged me to write a book I was sure no university press would want to publish and who supported me all the way. Many thanks as well to John Puckett and József Litkei for their enthusiasm and excellent work. The Central European University proved to be a rallying institution in this time of crisis: Constantin Iordachi and Balázs Trencsényi at *East Central Europe* and Ferenc Laczó at *Review of Democracy* published articles of mine touching on Covid issues early on; András Bozóki generously offered to circulate one of my texts among his students to gain feedback; and Éloïse Adde graced me with her brilliant intellectual input. The CEU rocks! Thirty-five years after the fall of communism in Central Europe, the university is more than ever a beacon of critical reflection.

When the stars align, social media can be an appreciable tool for creating social fabric. Many people criticize Twitter as a purveyor of online hate, and this is doubtless true in many cases. But the platform also provides a uniquely democratic opportunity to bypass technocratic gatekeepers and communicate with anyone, no matter their social status. I have enjoyed this intellectual and human potential. Beyond a mostly friendly crowd which has engaged me in a number of fruitful debates, I have discovered new colleagues and sometimes made new friends, personalities who have welcomed critical perspectives on the Covid response with a heartwarming measure of humanity, grace, and intellectual support. A very special mention in this respect goes to Toby Green, Ian Solliec, Anthony LaMesa, Daniel Hadas, Ondřej Krátký, Jason Strecker, Kevin Bardosh, Maximilien Lacour, Thomas Fazi, Jenin Younes, and Jay Bhattacharya. Your kindness in these troubled times has meant more to me than I can express.

I dedicate this book to the courageous individuals, anonymous or famous, who stood up to peer pressure and authoritarianism, who never compromised on critical thinking, sometimes at great cost to their career, and who resisted the ambient dehumanization of others. As a historian of communism, I knew all, in theory, about the feeling of solidarity stemming from standing together as a small group against the rest of the world. But I never dreamed I would experience it firsthand one day. To the dissidents!

September 12, 2024

This book incorporates material from previously published works, which have informed and shaped its development. I have revised and expanded them into the broader scope and arguments presented here. They include:

- Blaive, Muriel. "(Literally) Scared to Death: The Urgency of a Balanced Debate about Covid." *Britské listy*, October 9, 2020, https://blisty.cz/art/101421-literally-scared-to-death.html.
- Blaive, Muriel. "Surveillance Society: From Communist Czechoslovakia to Contemporary Western Democracies." In *East Central Europe* 49, nos. 2–3 (October 2022): 254–75.
- Blaive, Muriel. "Illiberal Liberalism: Covid and the Moral Crisis of the Left." *Review of Democracy*, November 17, 2023, https://revdem.ceu.edu/2023/11/17/illiberal-liberalism-covid-and-the-moral-crisis-of-the-left/.
- Blaive, Muriel. "Censorship is unacceptable in democracies—It also disqualifies the 'We didn't know' argument," *Collateral Global*, February 8, 2024, https://collateralglobal.org/wp-content/uploads/2024/02/censorship-unacceptable-democracies.pdf.

Moreover, this work has been supported by the Austrian Science Fund (FWF) via Elise Richter grant no. V912-G. The FWF has also supported the Open Access policy for this volume with grant PUB 1183-P (DOI: 10.55776/PUB1183.) Many thanks to the FWF for this double support, as well as to the Sociology Department at the University of Graz and to my friend and colleague, Libora Oates-Indruchová.

Legal Disclaimer

This book provides a scholarly analysis of the Covid crisis that began in 2020. It is intended for research and reflection purposes only, and the views expressed are solely those of the author. Neither the author nor the publisher shall be held responsible for any unintended consequences arising from the information contained in this book, its sources, or any potential errors or omissions.

Every effort has been made to ensure the information is accurate and reliable at the time of publication. Any identified errors will be addressed in future editions.

Introduction

The Covid Response and the Erosion of Democracy

> The wrong view of science betrays itself in the craving to be right; for it is not his possession of knowledge, of irrefutable truth, that makes the man of science, but his persistent and recklessly critical quest for truth.
>
> Karl Popper, *The Logic of Scientific Discovery*

In March 2020, I was nonplussed by the manner in which many of my colleagues reacted to the unfolding crisis. Fellow scholars of communism embraced practices they had spent their careers criticizing: censorship, repression, and propaganda. Disturbingly, educated people proved adept at public shaming, at the weaponization of moral virtue, and at the dehumanization of those they disagreed with. Even though the existential aim of social sciences is debate and disagreement in order to further knowledge, a sudden groupthink repurposed debate and disagreement as the expression of would-be alt-right extremism.

This has to stop. Grounded criticism must be urgently restored within social sciences and public health without a potential critic incurring the risk of being delegitimized and public-shamed as a "supporter of Donald Trump." In France, philosopher Barbara Stiegler pointed out early in the pandemic that the fate of democracy depended on the respect for scientific discussion and on the ability of the academic world to be heard in political debates. Instead, President Macron's martial rhetoric, according to which France was at war with the virus, led to the "construction of a binary world opposing 'progressives' concerned with life and health 'whatever it may cost' and the 'populists' accused of denying the reality of the virus and supporting conspiracy theories."[1] In place of the required academic spirit, we reached the "end of discussion,"[2] or, as Chimamanda Ngozi Adichie put it in a slightly different context, the "end of curiosity."[3] The imaginary of an unprecedented event, which seemed to require an unprecedented response, had taken hold.[4] Fear now prevailed.

The aim of this short volume is to show that the end of discussion and the end of curiosity have allowed the Covid measures to simultaneously wreak havoc on public health and undermine the rule of law, which is why I argue that the art of debate must be urgently restored. Censorship is unethical, unscientific, and unproductive. It has led to self-censorship and has prevented us from assessing the opinion of the public as the events unfolded. But there is even more at stake today: not only is the anatomical deconstruction of the historical, social, and political context which presided over this "end of discussion" necessary on its own merits, but the way in which we will collectively manage to deal with a mistake of untold proportions, the lockdown, is almost as important as the mistake itself. If scientists and independent thinkers have been

---

1 See Radio France, "Barbara Stiegler, déconfiner l'esprit de la recherche," *France Culture*, October 28, 2021, https://www.radiofrance.fr/franceculture/podcasts/tracts-le-podcast/barbara-stiegler-6860305. See also her essay *De la démocratie en pandémie: santé, recherche, éducation* (Paris: Gallimard, 2021).

2 Radio France, "Barbara Stiegler."

3 Emma Sarappo, "Chimamanda Ngozi Adichie: 'I Worry That What We're Looking at Is the End of Curiosity,'" *The Atlantic*, October 2, 2023, https://www.theatlantic.com/books/archive/2023/10/chimamanda-ngozi-adichie-atlantic-festival-freedom-creativity/675513/.

4 Carlo Caduff, "What Went Wrong: Corona and the World after Full Stop," *Medical Anthropology Quarterly*, July 21, 2020, https://anthrosource.onlinelibrary.wiley.com/doi/10.1111/maq.12599.

attacked from all sides,[5] criticism of the botched pandemic response and the defense of free speech seem to have increasingly shifted to conservative, arch-conservative, and extreme right circles. Should the liberal left really desert this battlefield, it will put both itself and democracy in grave danger. Just like many interwar and postwar European intellectuals were obsessed with anti-fascism to the point of endorsing dictatorial communist regimes, today's intellectuals are so keen on performative outrage towards Donald Trump (or his equivalents in other countries) that they have ceased caring about preserving democracy. It is at this juncture that Covid appeared and became the pretext for a political fight that has gone far beyond a simple virus.

Many academics persist to this day in denying the symbolical importance of the way we threw democracy overboard in 2020, mainly because the vast majority of those who now intuitively grasp that they supported the wrong Covid narrative just do not want to acknowledge it, let alone apologize for it. They would rather claim that democracy is not worth defending than admit they were wrong in choosing not to defend it. They would rather finish sacrificing democracy than admit they were mistaken in their support of measures that were not only useless against Covid but harmful in all other regards and destructive of freedom. And the liberal media would rather forego the task of investigating the egregious financial interests around the Covid vaccine than admit they were wrong to support vaccine mandates.

It is this attitude which might well prove to be the last nail in the coffin of democracy.

---

5 See John Ioannidis, "How the Pandemic is Changing the Norms of Science," *Tablet*, September 9, 2021, https://www.tabletmag.com/sections/science/articles/pandemic-science.

The importance of criticism

"Winning the battle against the virus," noted Amnesty International already in 2021, "includes not just government-led actions but also bottom-up approaches, which can only come about if freedom of expression and access to information are enabled." In order to successfully fight back Covid, states should "inform, empower, and listen to communities."[6] However, governments had "curtailed freedom of expression instead of encouraging it."[7] Moreover, the humanities and social sciences were almost completely sidelined by narrow fields such as computational epidemiology.[8]

The "end of discussion" is the very opposite of science. In the established theory of knowledge, represented among others by Karl Popper, science should search for evidence which might *disconfirm* a theory, not confirm it. In other words, to put a theory to the test, one must look for contradictory evidence. Only pseudoscience looks for "proofs" that confirm the theory. It is indeed too easy to find them if one is deliberately looking for them; this is known as confirmation bias.[9] Since the only genuine test of a theory is the attempt to falsify it, a

---

6 Amnesty International, "Executive Summary," in "Silenced and Misinformed: Freedom of Expression in Danger during Covid-19," October 2021, 5, https://www.amnesty.org/en/documents/pol30/4751/2021/en/.

7 "Executive Summary," 5.

8 See Peter Sutoris and Sinéad Murphy, "The Role of Humanities and Social Sciences at a Time of Crisis," in *Pandemic Response and the Cost of Lockdowns: Global Debates from Humanities and Social Sciences*, ed. Peter Sutoris, Sinéad Murphy, Aleida Mendes Borges, Yossi Nehushtan (London: Routledge, 2023), 1. Daniel Briggs and Toby Green stressed the same issue in a podcast of Collateral Global, "Lockdown Social Harms in the Covid Era," YouTube video, 40:29, December 15, 2021, https://www.youtube.com/watch?v=Hnto821P0Kg.

9 See Karl Popper, *The Open Society and Its Enemies* (London: Routledge, 1945). For a condensed explanation, see Philosophy Overdose, "Karl Popper on Science and Absolute Truth (1974)," YouTube video, 6:22, https://www.youtube.com/watch?v=li0ciaqJ0m0. See also the excellent Crash Course on "Karl Popper, Science, and Pseudoscience: Crash Course Philosophy No. 8," YouTube video, 8:56, March 28, 2016, https://www.youtube.com/watch?v=-X8Xfl0JdTQ.

contradictory debate is crucial. Theories which are irrefutable are unscientific by principle. In other words, certainty is the opposite of science; what science requires is to let go of beliefs and accept the evidence which disproves the theory. We can thus infer that censorship, which prevents the possibility of refuting a theory, is enough to turn a theory unscientific.

The most serious scientific challenge to the official Covid narrative in the West, outside of Sweden, was the Great Barrington Declaration. In October 2020, Sunetra Gupta (Oxford), Jay Bhattacharya (Stanford), and Martin Kulldorff (Harvard) co-authored an open letter which argued that the Covid lockdowns were harmful. They advocated focused protection for those most at risk from the virus, while the young and healthy should continue to lead a normal life. This was the policy pursued by Sweden's head epidemiologist, Anders Tegnell. Although signed by many health professionals, the Great Barrington Declaration was denounced as dangerous and unscientific by the World Health Organization and health authorities in most Western countries. The director of the American National Institutes of Health (NIH), Francis Collins, demanded its "quick and devastating takedown."[10]

What was taken down, however, was not the Declaration itself but the chance to hold a productive scientific debate. We now know that Sweden achieved the lowest or one of the lowest excess mortalities in the developed world during the period 2020-2022.[11] The "illusion of consensus," an expression coined by sociologist Chantal Mouffe according to which it is

10 Editorial board, "How Fauci and Collins Shut Down the Covid Debate. They Worked with the Media to Trash the Great Barrington Declaration," *Wall Street Journal*, December 21, 2021, https://www.wsj.com/articles/fauci-collins-emails-great-barrington-declaration-covid-pandemic-lockdown-11640129116.

11 According to Statistics Sweden, see Therese Bergstedt, "Anders Tegnell: gillar inte ordet 'revansch,'" *Svenska Dagbladet*, March 4, 2023, https://www.svd.se/a/JQvVnj/anders-tegnell-efter-pandemin-overdodlighet-ger-inte-hela-svaret—see the discussion of the figures in Chapter 1.

conceptually wrong and politically dangerous to conceive of democracy as a "consensus,"[12] now became the title of a podcast hosted by GBD co-author Jay Bhattacharya.[13] This illusory consensus was the cornerstone of a Covid policy which influenced public opinion as any consensus does,[14] yet was by definition unscientific or, as Popper would put it, pseudoscientific, and turned out to be wrong. The would-be consensus was the sign of a closed society, not of an open, democratic one. The "Covid doxa," as sociologist Laurent Mucchielli put it, was a semantic matrix which mainly served to have the public adhere to an explanation of events. In reality, this dominant discourse served to protect the social order, i.e., to provide a theoretical justification for the domination of the privileged.[15]

One of this volume's aims is to try and understand why so many people, even among academics, endorsed this pseudo-consensus and proved incapable of questioning official policies and challenging this intellectual dominance.[16] American social scientists in particular appear so politically paralyzed by the fear of providing intellectual ammunition to Donald Trump that to this day, they have hardly published any social

---

12 See Chantal Mouffe, *L'illusion du consensus* (Paris: Albin Michel, 2016). Many thanks to Éloïse Adde for the reference.

13 See Jay Bhattacharya and Martin Kulldorff, "Martin Kulldorff on why he was fired from Harvard," *The Illusion of Consensus* (podcast), https://www.illusionconsensus.com/p/must-watch-episode-36-martin-kulldorff.

14 Sander L. van der Linden, Chris E. Clarke, and Edward W. Maibach, "Highlighting Consensus among Medical Scientists Increases Public Support for Vaccines: Evidence from a Randomized Experiment," *BMC Public Health*, December 3, 2015, https://www.ncbi.nlm.nih.gov/pmc/articles/PMC4669673/.

15 Laurent Mucchielli, "The Covid Doxa: How Propaganda, Censorship, and the Politicization of Covid Have Destroyed Our Intellectual and Moral Bearings," *Kritische Gesellschaftsforschung (Critical Society Studies)*, no. 2, 2023, https://www.kritischegesellschaftsforschung.de/Journal/Article/65/50/pdf.

16 See the scholars of Africa Toby Green and Reginald Oduor in dialogue with Jay Bhattacharya in "Is the New WHO Treaty Neo-Colonialism in Public Health Disguise?" *The Illusion of Consensus* (podcast), April 6, 2024, https://www.illusionconsensus.com/p/ep-44-who-treaty.

science volume critically analyzing the Covid response, as opposed to French and even more so British scholars; standard English publishing houses such as Routledge, Palgrave Macmillan, and Bristol University Press now routinely publish critical views of the pandemic response.

From lockdown to crackdown

I have felt it both a right and a duty to question the soundness and merits of our Covid policies, but as with anyone who dared speaking out, it was immediately implied on Facebook by my own friends and colleagues that I must be a crackpot conspiracy theorist, antivaxxer, or white supremacist. I am fully vaccinated against Covid, as are my parents and my children, and this book is anyway not about the Covid vaccine. But I am not vaccinated against exercising critical thinking. The widespread assumption according to which any critic must be a lunatic has been extremely detrimental, indeed catastrophic to public health and democracy.[17] Indeed, as predicted, we went from lockdown to crackdown. Some colleagues privately agreed with me but did not dare to say so publicly for fear of wreaking their careers. The "scientific truth" was what people believed in, as if scientists were not saying everything and its contrary in all sincerity, as if their debates were devoid of political issues, personal rivalries, economic interests, and power struggles, as if this intangible scientific truth excluded the need for further discussion, and as if it did not evolve every so often.

17 Kevin Bass, "It's Time for the Scientific Community to Admit We Were Wrong about COVID and It Cost Lives," *Newsweek*, January 30, 2023, https://www.newsweek.com/its-time-scientific-community-admit-we-were-wrong-about-coivd-it-cost-lives-opinion-1776630. As a result of this article, the author, a medical student, was expelled from the School of Medicine at Texas Tech University, see his story here: Kevin Bass, "How My Medical School Scandalously Dismissed Me," *The Illusion of Consensus* (podcast), February 2, 2024, https://www.illusionconsensus.com/p/how-my-medical-school-scandalously.

Any form of criticism was understood as tantamount to the betrayal of human decency. Irrationality became the order of the day on both sides of the political spectrum. On one extreme, some persist to this day in denying that Covid even exists. In the opposite camp, vaccinated people started to catch Covid (so-called breakthrough infections) but pronounced themselves grateful to be vaccinated otherwise the course of their disease would be "so much worse." They did not contemplate the fact that catching a disease while being fully vaccinated against it should probably be considered a sign of vaccine failure rather than success. We can hardly imagine people repeatedly catching polio while vaccinated against it to be grateful, otherwise, their polio cases would be "so much worse." And what to think of the people who wore a mask to swim or while driving alone in their cars?

A cross-section of the population, primarily amongst the liberal left, entertained mainstream media and social media for years with dramatic and angry denunciations of the would-be culprits who had contaminated them. They seemed convinced that the virus could be defeated by civic virtue if only everyone behaved in the required careful manner, and if they themselves had not let their guard down for a fateful moment. And when they did catch Covid, they were convinced their life was saved only thanks to Paxlovid and they were grateful to science, in which they "believed."[18]

These pundits would be surprised to hear that in Europe and elsewhere, access to Paxlovid was restricted due to unavailability and also due to its eye-watering price that even European health insurances couldn't always afford. As a result, hundreds of millions of people outside American

18 Candy Schulman, "You Finally Got Me, Covid, after All I Did to Avoid You: Two Years Ago, I Would Have Been terrified. Now I'm Mostly Just Angry," *The Washington Post*, July 14, 2022, https://www.washingtonpost.com/outlook/2022/07/14/covid-new-york-paxlovid/.

liberal circles overcame Covid even without its would-be precious help. Price is not always a sign of quality or indispensableness; on the other hand, it is the sure sign of a pharmaceutical company getting very rich—for as long as a given society "believes in science" anyway.[19]

Sources and methodology

I use as a main source mainstream media articles, typically the *Guardian*, the *New York Times*, and the *Washington Post*, but also public debates as they were reported in mainstream media and social media, including on my Facebook wall and Twitter feed, where I am quite active. I also make use of scientific literature, but sparingly so, as this volume mainly focuses on the evolution of the public debate and is destined as much to the wider public as to the academic community. When possible, I cite a podcast or a mainstream media article rather than an academic volume.

My methodology is a mixture of ethnography, participant observation, and action research. It is ethnographical in the sense that I commence from the study of a specific social group, community, and culture of academia through immersive involvement, and autoethnographic in the sense that I situate myself within this narrative. It is socio-historical, as I use both my insider's perspective on the culture, behavior, and social dynamics of Western public intellectuals, mainly scholars of communism, and my knowledge of communist history. And it is a form of action research in the sense that my approach is both reflexive and participatory: I have been

19 Bhanvi Satija and Michael Erman, "Pfizer Looks Beyond COVID after Quarterly Loss on Paxlovid Charge," *Reuters*, October 23, 2023, https://www.reuters.com/business/healthcare-pharmaceuticals/pfizer-swings-quarterly-loss-due-paxlovid-write-off-2023-10-31/.

in turn acting, observing, and reflecting, aiming all at once to bring about change (the abolition of censorship) and to analyze what the conditions for such change are and why it has not always been possible to push it through. For this volume, I christen this method sociocultural reflexive engagement.

Being French while living in Austria and working on Czech history but having most of my friends and colleagues in the US has led me to follow events in these specific countries more closely. My initial, offhand notes evolved into this concise historical and biopolitical analysis and contextualization of the reception and handling of Covid.

Medicine is not an exact science: An autoethnographic introduction

Several elements in my relationship to the medical world account for my spontaneously critical reaction to the official Covid response. However, as mentioned above, just like anyone who dared question the official Covid response, I was publicly delegitimized for my absence of medical expertise, with arguments such as "You're not a doctor, so how can you know," as if a number of doctors did not also have a dissenting opinion from the official narrative. Many people, even in academia, thought any critic was most probably a sort of esoteric charlatan who "does not believe in science."

As it happens, both my parents are medical doctors, and my grandfather was a hospital director. But what growing up surrounded by white blouses paradoxically taught me is that medicine is far from being an exact science. My parents passionately argued at mealtimes over various patients' cases and were, of course, always convinced they were right against the other. What united them is that they were both convinced they were right against any outside layperson, who could not possibly hold a relevant expert opinion since he or she was no "scientist" as opposed to them.

My father had something of a reputation as a physician. He was occasionally contacted by the media for interviews and treated with the customary deference reserved for the figure of the medical demigod. This admiration on the side of the interviewer unfailingly extended to wider topics as the conversation moved on, and I could always pinpoint the exact moment in which my father was led out of his field of expertise to improvise answers to questions which he was neither familiar with nor felt competent about—answers that sometimes greatly surprised me, and perhaps even himself. I instantly recognized this pattern when countless doctors were interviewed during the pandemic.

I spent much time in my father's hospital as I was growing up, and I made great use of the fact that nearly all doors were open to me as the boss's daughter. As I wanted to become a physician, too (I even enrolled in the medical faculty before opting at the last minute for political science), my eyes and ears were wide open. But what I observed chiefly was that the patient was an abstract and somewhat dehumanized category. Not that the medical personnel, including my father, were not kind to the patients—they were. But people were precisely seen as patients, not as individuals with a history, their own experiences, beliefs, and approaches to their own diseases. The idea that a patient might have an autonomous opinion about his or her condition and treatment was, here too, anathema.

I also witnessed the death of my grandmother in this very same hospital department. On this occasion I could appreciate, on the contrary, the incompetence and cowardice of the inexperienced personnel who were on duty that particular night, so terrified of an old woman dying that they ran away and left me to cope alone with her painful agony. Incompetent and unempathetic medical personnel are, alas, as indisputable a fact of life in hospitals as competent and humane ones.[20] I did note, however, how comforting it was for both my grandmother and me to be together in her last moment. To let Covid patients die alone, far from their families, on the pretext that they risked transmitting the disease even though they had often lived with their families until the ambulance came, is one of the most inhumane aspects of the pandemic management. Despite cries that we implemented stringent lockdowns to save our elderly parents, we proved remarkably indifferent to their loneliness. In order to "protect" them, we let them live their last months, weeks, or days alone, die alone, and even be buried alone.[21]

The pharmaceutical industry was already present in the second half of the 1980s in this provincial French hospital. The level of corruption, though, if such should be the word, was still rather innocuous; rather, the groundwork was prepared for future use. The medical visitor was happily greeted by the small personnel upon his or her regular visit; he or she extended a few goodies, donated boxes of the medicine

20 For an eloquent description of a certain culture of contempt of the patient in French medical circles, see the novels of physician Martin Winckler, for instance this one on gynecological and obstetrical violence on the part of colleagues that he often names "the butchers": *Le choeur des femmes* (Paris: POL, 2009). Another physician/novelist, Baptiste Beaulieu, also documented the systemic suppression of emotions amongst French medical professionals: Alice Raybaud, "Baptiste Beaulieu, médecin et écrivain: 'Le milieu medical nous demande de ne pas exprimer nos émotions,'" *Le Monde*, October 8, 2021, https://www.lemonde.fr/campus/article/2021/10/08/baptiste-beaulieu-medecin-et-ecrivain-le-milieu-medical-nous-demande-de-ne-pas-exprimer-nos-emotions_6097579_4401467.html. For similar, hair-raising American examples, see Marty Makary, *Blind Spots: When Medicine Gets It Wrong, and What It Means for Our Health* (New York: Bloomsbury, 2024).

21 This dreadful phenomenon of social exclusion was also analyzed in Daniel Briggs, Luke Telford, Anthony Lloyd, and Anthony Ellis, *The New Futures of Exclusion: Life in the Covid-19 Aftermath* (London: Palgrave-Macmillan, 2023).

they were promoting, and invited those present for a lunch in the hospital café while exchanging the latest gossip. In fact, pharmaceutical companies were popular, because they played in those years an essential role of information and socialization at a time when the central research agency (CNRS) seemed unapproachable to hospitals which were far from the Parisian power circles, while European research funds were not available yet. As for universities, which are mostly public in France, they had little or no money and still don't. Before pharma became big pharma, it thus fulfilled an essential role of funding research projects in provincial hospitals, bringing regional physicians to international congresses when no other source of funding existed, and starting in the 1990s, ushering in a truly global dimension by bringing together scientists from all over the world, including developing countries. In other words, it fulfilled for a few decades the role that state research institutions took on only later.

At the beginning of the 1990s, my father was invited by a pharmaceutical company to an international medical congress, as he was almost every year. As my mother couldn't go, he took me instead. We traveled economy, but we were accommodated in what seemed to me a luxurious hotel. My father apparently knew everyone there, just like I know everyone at the international congresses which I frequent today. We, the "spouses," were taken care of on that occasion and given a three-day tour of the environs while the scientists were at work. I asked my father if he felt compelled by this fancy invitation to prescribe more of the drugs produced by the pharmaceutical company in question. Not at all, he told me—if the company was naive enough to believe they could buy his services with such an invitation, they were sorely mistaken, as he strictly prescribed to the patient what he felt was right for them. We laughed. But were all physicians as incorruptible as my father?

Timing (things started to change dramatically in the 1990s), geography, and scale are at stake here. In the US, between 2013 and 2022, more than $12 billion were distributed by the pharmaceutical industry to physicians. In practical terms, this meant that 57% of American physicians received money from the industry; in 93% of the cases, this involved a marketed medical product: "Payments varied widely between specialties and between physicians within the same specialty. A small number of physicians received the largest amounts, often exceeding $1 million, while the median physician received much less, typically less than a hundred dollars."[22]

Who can believe that there is no conflict of interest at stake in many cases here? I was not surprised that John le Carré's first post-Cold War story, *The Constant Gardener* (2001), concerned an egregious corruption and criminal case involving the pharmaceutical industry. Money flowed in the medical field on an exponential scale starting in the 1990s. This led me to wonder whether the opinions on Covid matters we received during the pandemic were skewed in a similar manner, all the more so that a long series of public health scandals in France served as warning for me, with lessons easily applicable to Covid.

The long history of public health scandals in France: A warning

I was attuned to the fact that France has known a number of medical and biopolitical scandals in the past decades. We were taught in school that the French nuclear tests which

22 Ahmed Sayed, Joseph S. Ross, and John Mendrola, "Industry Payments to U.S. Physicians by Specialty and Product Type," *JAMA*, March 28, 2024, https://jamanetwork.com/journals/jama/fullarticle/2816900?guestAccessKey=fd-8da7dc-c8bd-4913-96c4-9bd5d537299a.

took place in the French Pacific islands in the 1960s and 1970s held the health of the local populations in utter disregard, even though the dangers of exposure were already well known. The local population and military failed to be indemnified for years for the damage caused to their health; soldiers overseeing the nuclear tests wore shorts and t-shirts as their only cover and were only told not to look at the explosion but to lie flat on the ground. French courts refused until 2008 to compensate any victim, and when they finally did, it was only very sparingly.[23]

While I was in high school in the US in 1985-86 for a one-year student exchange, I was surprised to see on the map shown on American television that the whole of Europe, including France, was contaminated by the Chernobyl nuclear cloud, even though my mother assured me on the phone that French news reported the cloud to have stopped over the French border.[24] Despite the calls of numerous whistleblowers in the medical world after what they saw as a suspicious increase of thyroid cancers, neither French authorities nor French courts have ever recognized the damage caused by the lack of recommendations (mushrooms were consumed normally and children allowed to play in sand pitches, for instance, as opposed to nearly all neighboring countries).[25]

A number of public health scandals followed over the years, for instance, that of Dépakine, a medicine used to treat

---

23 Angelique Chrisafis, "French Nuclear Tests Showered Vast Areas of Polynesia with Radioactivity," *The Guardian*, July 3, 2013, https://www.theguardian.com/world/2013/jul/03/french-nuclear-tests-polynesia-declassified.

24 Judith Miller, "Trying to Quell a Furor, France Forms a Panel on Chernobyl," *The New York Times*, May 14, 1986, https://www.nytimes.com/1986/05/14/world/trying-to-quell-a-furor-france-forms-a-panel-on-chernobyl.html.

25 "French Court Dismisses Chernobyl Nuclear Fallout Case after 10 Years," *Radio France Internationale*, September 7, 2011, https://www.rfi.fr/en/asia-pacific/20110907-french-court-dismisses-chernobyl-nuclear-fallout-case-after-10-years.

epilepsy which pregnant women were allowed to take and which led to thousands of babies born with birth defects, including physical and psychological problems. In the UK, too, 20,000 babies were born with deformities because of this drug, yet pregnant women were still prescribed it as late as in 2022.[26] The French medicine agency, as well as the pharmaceutical company which produces the medicine, Sanofi, were indicted in a class action suit in 2020, a trial which is still pending (the French justice system is very slow). So far, only two families have won a trial against Sanofi.[27] When the vaccine against Covid was prescribed to pregnant women as soon as it came out, despite the fact that it had not yet been tested at scale on pregnant women[28] and despite the fact that pregnant women were by definition not in the age bracket that was the most susceptible to die from Covid, I remembered the Dépakine scandal. However, this is the kind of debate which is silenced in France on the pretext that any doubt must amount to "disinformation."[29]

26 Cécile Ducourtieux, "In the UK, 20,000 Babies Have Been Born with Deformities Because of Misinformation about a Drug," *Le Monde*, April 21, 2022, https://www.lemonde.fr/en/international/article/2022/04/21/in-the-uk-20-000-babies-have-been-born-with-deformities-because-of-misinformation-about-a-drug_5981177_4.html.

27 "Affaire de la Dépakine: Sanofi condamné à indemniser une famille à hauteur de 450 000 euros pour manque d'informations sur la notice," *France Info*, May 14, 2022, https://www.francetvinfo.fr/sante/grossesse/depakine/affaire-de-la-depakine-sanofi-condamne-a-indemniser-une-famille-a-hauteur-de-450-000-euros-pour-manque-d-informations-sur-la-notice_5138155.html. See also Catherine Fournier, "Sanofi condamné dans l'affaire: Dépakine pourquoi ce jugement est particulièrement important, notamment pour les victimes," *France Info*, September 9, 2024, https://www.francetvinfo.fr/sante/grossesse/depakine/sanofi-condamne-dans-l-affaire-depakine-pourquoi-ce-jugement-est-particulierement-important-notamment-pour-les-victimes_6775228.html.

28 Julie Steenhuysen, "Large U.S. Covid-19 Vaccine Trials will Exclude Pregnant Women for Now," *Reuters*, July 31, 2020, https://www.reuters.com/article/idUSKCN24W1NY/.

29 See Marine Martin, *Dépakine: le scandale. Je ne pouvais pas me taire* (Paris: Robert Laffont, 2017).

Among a number of other health scandals in France concerning medicines with severe or fatal side effects (Vioxx, Médiator), which all involved an extremely slow reaction of the French health authorities (typically years, if not decades) as well as adamant denials on the part of the pharmaceutical industry, a pesticide called Chlordécone was used in banana plantations in the French Caribbean islands of Martinique and Guadeloupe for approximately twenty years in the 1970s and 1980s. Although banned in the US since 1976, it was legally used in France until 1993, and a lawsuit concluded in 2023, against the opinion of a number of experts and to the indignation of the local population, that its hazardous nature was not proven. Yet, this highly toxic product is now found in the blood of 90% of the Martiniquais and Guadeloupeans, and the prevalence of prostate cancer in the region is the highest in the world.[30] An expert interviewed by French public radio claimed that already in the 1970s "from the scientific literature we knew 80% of what we know today about the toxicity of this product,"[31] which explains why the US banned it at that time.

If, for once, authorities took the Covid pandemic seriously enough,[32] French mainstream media stopped being sympathetic to the same island natives when the latter displayed suspicion and distrust toward the Covid vaccine, presented

30 Anne-Laure Barral, "Scandale de la chlordécone: de nouveaux éléments contredisent la justice," *France Inter*, April 21, 2023, https://www.radiofrance.fr/franceinter/scandale-de-la-chlordecone-de-nouveaux-elements-contredisent-la-justice-1339660.

31 Barral, "Scandale de la chlordécone." See also Faustine Vincent, "Scandale sanitaire aux Antilles: qu'est-ce que le chlordécone?" *Le Monde*, June 6, 2017, https://www.lemonde.fr/planete/article/2018/06/06/scandale-sanitaire-aux-antilles-qu-est-ce-que-le-chlordecone_5310485_3244.html.

32 Slavoj Žižek rightly objected to Giorgio Agamben that, this time at least, the authorities had taken the danger seriously. See Slavoj Žižek, "Monitor and Punish? Yes, Please!" *The Philosophical Salon*, March 16, 2020, https://thephilosophicalsalon.com/monitor-and-punish-yes-please/.

yet again as "100% safe and effective" by the central state. Can the local population be blamed for feeling suspicious, especially knowing that, if history was any guide, a potential trial would likely turn against them? Part of the health personnel went on strike when the vaccine was made mandatory. But in a barely disguised contempt that smacked of racism for the (largely black) inhabitants of the Antilles, implicitly presented as not quite as civilized as the rest of France, the reluctance of the local population to take the vaccine was blamed on "local beliefs," as well as on "illiteracy, poverty," and, only then, "Chlordécone."[33]

Finally, yet another egregious case of health mismanagement in France was the so-called "contaminated blood" scandal. When AIDS first appeared and developed in the US at the beginning of the 1980s, medical authorities suspected within a couple of years that the virus was transmitted not only by sexual contact but also by blood, which was a conundrum for hemophiliacs. The multiple rivalries between authorities in the regional blood collection centers and the central state, the complex financial interests of the French state versus American firms which were more advanced in the treatment of AIDS, and a widespread political and medical incompetence and shortsightedness all combined to have approximately half of the 4,000 French hemophiliacs infected by AIDS, half of whom died from it, which was a much worse record than other European countries.[34] But the scandal did not stop there: although families were initially financially compensated at a small level (100,000 francs per victim, i.e., approximately

33 Hugues Garnier, "Défiance, croyances locales: pourquoi le vaccin contre le Covid-19 est boudé en Martinique," *BFM TV*, August 2, 2021, https://www.bfmtv.com/sante/defiance-croyances-locales-pourquoi-le-vaccin-contre-le-covid-19-est-boude-en-martinique_AV-202108020129.html.

34 See the Wikipedia page "Affaire du sang contaminé," which is very detailed and well documented: https://fr.wikipedia.org/wiki/Affaire_du_sang_contamin%C3%A9.

15,000 euros, which was very little even in those days), and although two officials were originally sent to jail for two years, all health authorities, from the most local to the prime minister, thirty officials in all, were eventually cleared of any wrongdoing in 2003 by the highest French court, the Cour de cassation.[35] The public outcry was immense.[36]

I saw the TV interview on November 3, 1991, of the former Minister of Social Affairs, Georgina Dufoix, who declared, as the scandal started to bloom, that she felt "responsible but not guilty" ("responsable mais pas coupable"[37]), which became a national joke in France, repeated when officials commit blunders (that are almost never punished), "Oh, so he/she is responsible but not guilty…." It taught me and many other French citizens to always be critical of state narratives on public health. As to Britain, it was even slower in dealing with its own contaminated blood victims since the case is still ongoing, but at least the victims are now projected to receive from £2.2 to £2.6 million each.[38]

I returned to my interest in medical matters when I led a three-year research project in the 2010s on the social and medical practices of childbirth in the Soviet bloc compared with the US. I never had a chance to finish my project and publish the book I was planning, or even some articles, because I became entangled towards the end of my project in a political fight in Prague for the control of the Institute for the Study

35 "La clôture définitive de l'affaire du sang contaminé," *lexbase.fr*, June 20, 2003, https://www.lexbase.fr/revues-juridiques/3215014-jurisprudencelacloturedefinitivedelaffairedusangcontamine.

36 "La justice met fin à l'affaire du sang contaminé," *Le Monde*, June 18, 2003, https://www.lemonde.fr/archives/article/2003/06/18/la-justice-met-fin-a-l-affaire-du-sang-contamine_324422_1819218.html.

37 "Mme Dufoix s'estime 'responsable' mais pas 'coupable,'" *Le Monde*, November 4, 1991, https://www.lemonde.fr/archives/article/1991/11/05/mme-dufoix-s-estime-responsable-mais-pas-coupable_4033131_1819218.html.

38 Jim Reed, "What is the Infected Blood Scandal and Will Victims Get Compensation?" *BBC*, May 21, 2024, https://www.bbc.com/news/health-48596605.

of Totalitarian Regimes, where I then worked until 2022, so this historical medical project is still on standby. But I did spend three years reading the relevant medical and sociological literature, and I became fully appraised of the challenges of biopolitics, i.e., of the attempt by authorities to control the bodies of their citizens, in this case via the medical profession. I made note of the American tendency to overmedicalize any health issue, in this case childbirth, as the health sector has always been primarily private, and physicians make more money if they perform more medical procedures. This led to an inflation of the number of cesarian sections in the US compared to Europe. I was reminded of this unique heavy-handed bias when Governor Cuomo demanded 40,000 ventilators for New York alone in April 2020—incidentally, it later turned out that these ventilators were more dangerous than useful, and they were soon abandoned as standard treatment.

Medicine is also embedded in national culture

My permanently "critical medical attitude" also stems from the fact that I have been living abroad, meaning outside of France, since 1992. I could observe for decades, in both Prague and Vienna, how medical practices are embedded in national culture and how medical protocols, predicated on local interpretations of what "science" is, can be contradictory from country to country. For instance, where my mother prescribed me antibiotics, Austrian doctors would be much more reluctant and recommend waiting for a few days. While I was firmly convinced in the first years of my emigration that the French medical approach was the only right one, in due time I came to appreciate that the Czech and Austrian ways had their merits, too—indeed, to my own surprise, I did not immediately die when I did not strictly follow my mother's prescriptions.

I came to see that medicine is in large part a cultural practice and that we should not necessarily believe every word a physician ever says but compare and contrast with other medical opinions and other medical methodologies.

The last element of my medical experience which had a great influence on my understanding of the Covid crisis in March 2020 is that I had been suffering from a stage IV melanoma since January 2015. For one thing, the two dermatologists I had consulted in the two or three years prior to my diagnosis had assured me that my itchy and bleeding mole was "nothing." Even the intern who reluctantly took a biopsy of my swollen lymph nodes was convinced it was useless and profusely apologized when he handed me the results. Misdiagnosis is a frequent reality; the word of doctors is not necessarily "the truth." And for another thing, as opposed to most people, I was already accustomed to the idea of suddenly dying from an unpredictable disease. This is also why to accuse me of not trusting medical protocols and revolutionary medicines (in my case, immunotherapy) is absurd, as they literally saved my life only a few years ago. More relevant is that I was still in need of some therapy (blood and iron infusions) in 2020 for a persistent anemia, yet I was kicked out of the Vienna General Hospital in March to make space for putative Covid patients and to "limit infections."[39] I experienced as a terrible betrayal that my treatment was interrupted all the way until 2021 and that it took several years for normal medical procedures to resume at the hospital. Also in France, hospitals have still not fully recovered.[40]

39 See Muriel Blaive, "(Literally) Scared to Death. The Urgency of a Balanced Debate about Covid," *Britské listy*, October 9, 2020, https://blisty.cz/art/101421-literally-scared-to-death.html.

40 Solenne Le Hen, "Covid-19: quatre ans après, les hôpitaux français ont retrouvé 'au global' leur niveau d'activité d'avant-crise, mais avec des 'disparités préoccupantes,'" *France Info*, March 8, 2024, https://www.francetvinfo.fr/sante/maladie/coronavirus/confinement/info-franceinfo-covid-19-quatre-ans-

To this day, neither the medical nor political authorities in Austria have reckoned with their actions during Covid. But artists and public opinion have done so: the director of the Vienna Festival, Milo Rau, put together a 20-hour mock trial of the Austrian leaders' handling of the Covid response, which left little doubt that the public received the Covid response as authoritarian, inefficient, extremely costly, and highly detrimental to children and to public health.[41] An association of Covid vaccine injury victims also organizes well-frequented gallery exhibits in public places.[42]

To sum up, what conditioned my urge to ask questions as the pandemic unfolded instead of taking our various policies for granted was that medicine is not an exact science; treatments must in any case be pondered and socially negotiated; and the priority given to Covid patients against any other type of patients was doomed to result in severe collateral damage.

So much for my "not believing in science." On the other hand, if democracy is a good and necessary system, then censorship as a cornerstone of the Covid response was extremely damaging and unethical. Its only result was to replace productive disagreement with ontological denial and dehumanization.

Dehumanization became a political argument

Communist history shows that the political posture which consists in restricting the freedom of speech of critics is not a potent way to seduce the population in the long term, as

apres-les-hopitaux-francais-ont-retrouve-au-global-leur-niveau-d-activite-d-avant-crise-mais-avec-des-disparites-preoccupantes_6430231.html.

41 Joëlle Stolz, "Au festival de Vienne, le 'procès' du Covid," *Le Club de Mediapart*, May 26, 2024, https://blogs.mediapart.fr/joelle-stolz/blog/260524/au-festival-de-vienne-le-proces-du-covid. Many thanks to Blaise Gauquelin for this reference.

42 See, for instance, a video of an exhibit on Vienna's Stephansplatz at the heart of the city on August 24, 2024, https://www.impfopfer.info/impfopfer-galerie-wien-am-24-august-2024/.

it only favors conspiracy theories while social discontent, if there is any, will manifest itself no matter the official narrative. A much better way to fight Covid deniers would have been to insist on debate and discussion, to think critically, to refute the pitching of "us" against "them." Thinking critically means systematically challenging the established truth and taking nothing for granted; it does not mean silencing the people who express any form of dissent on the pretext that they talk like the opposite camp or that they put the public in danger by raising its critical awareness. What has put the public, or more generally democracy, in danger has been to hold monologues, on both sides.

The neo-totalitarian frame of mind equally shared on the right and on the left has reframed any political disagreement as an ontological issue. It has only served to instill in society the belief that the opposing party deserves no less than dehumanization, while division and rejection of dissenting opinions is the proper way to lead public debate. Or rather, there is no need to lead a public debate anymore, since one's camp unfailingly holds "the truth" and the opposing camp must be silenced.

This is why it is crucial to reestablish a sphere in which it is safe to be neither a "leftist" nor a "populist," but a critical citizen who reasons independently of politics.

In order to do this in this volume, Chapter 1 delves into the way in which the normalization of fear and social compliance has laid the groundwork before and during Covid for what some call "digital authoritarianism." Chapter 2 explores the collateral damage wrought by lockdowns and censorship, using my own experience of Facebook censorship as a case study in biopolitical issues. In Chapter 3, I examine the instrumentalization of science and expertise during the pandemic. Chapter 4 assesses the detrimental impact of Covid policies on our democratic institutions, advocating for an urgent reassessment. And lastly, the conclusion scrutinizes the response of liberals to Covid, framing it in fact as a manifestation of illiberalism, and probes the pandemic as a moral and intellectual crisis for the liberal left.

Chapter 1

Laying the Groundwork for "Digital Authoritarianism": Social Compliance and the Normalization of Fear

> There is no need for a man who criticizes democracy and democratic institutions to be their enemy, although both the democrats he criticizes and the totalitarians who hope to profit from a disunion in the democratic camp are likely to brand him as such. There is a fundamental difference between a democratic and a totalitarian criticism of democracy.... Democrats who don't see the difference between a hostile and a friendly criticism of democracy are themselves imbued with the totalitarian spirit.
>
> Karl Popper, *The Open Society and Its Enemies*

As mentioned in the introduction, I'm a historian of communism and post-communism by trade and learned several useful lessons applicable to any social situation, including Covid, in the course of my historical work. I studied first the 1950s in Czechoslovakia and specifically wondered why no 1956 revolution on the Polish or Hungarian model took place there.[1] I concluded that the better standard of living and a genuine measure of support for the communist regime were the principal factors accounting for the different reaction of Czech and Slovak society. I then studied everyday life

1 See Muriel Blaive, *Une déstalinisation manquée: Tchécoslovaquie 1956* (Brussels: Complexe, 2005).

in a small Czech town at the foot of the Iron Curtain and showed that the regime enforced a mixture of repression and reward and that society could thus be simultaneously a victim of the regime and complicit in its maintenance, while most people just tried to live as normal a life as they could while compromising themselves as little as possible (although they still had to).[2] And finally, I studied the policy of dealing with the communist past in the post-communist Czech Republic[3] and showed that history can be rewritten at ease even in a democracy in order to fulfill the narrative the state wants to impose—in this case, a narrative of victimhood and anticommunism—while it could have just as easily been a history of passive acceptance and collaboration.

A pillar of authoritarian rule: Censorship

All three research contexts delineate ideology as a major policy drive, and, unsurprisingly, the standard of living is always a key factor in explaining the reaction of the population. But even more to the point, my own and other studies of society under communism show that censorship and surveillance are two characteristics of communist rule that were central and particularly pernicious. After the first phase of terror until 1953 (Stalinism), communist rule depended upon the threat of repression rather than on repression itself. Forced but also voluntary collaboration with the secret police paradoxically led society to surveil itself and to internalize this

2 See Muriel Blaive, "'The Cold War? I Have it at Home with My Family.' Memories of the 1948-1989 Period beyond the Iron Curtain," in *The Cold War: Historiography, Memory, Representation*, ed. Konrad Jarausch, Christian Ostermann, and Andreas Etges (Mouton: De Gruyter, 2017), 203–23.

3 See Muriel Blaive, "Codeword 'Criminal': Moral Remembrance in National Memory Politics," in *2020 State of the Region Report: Constructions and Instrumentalization of the Past; A Comparative Study on Memory Management in the Region*, ed. Ninna Mörner (Stockholm: Södertörn University, 2021), 106–14.

form of repression. Once the snitches were in place, the people policed one another, and the security services reaped the benefits of denunciation as a mass social practice. The parallel with the Covid response, when the police in lockdown nations were overwhelmed with denunciations, leaps to the eye.[4]

Censorship and afferent self-censorship are pillars of authoritarian rule under any regime, not just communism. Control of information suppresses dissent, enforces ideological conformity, manipulates the media, enables surveillance and fear, and is magnified by technological control. Irony abounds in the fact that the communist secret police had at least to trouble itself installing microphones in people's homes, while we buy them and install them on our own (Alexa, Echo, Google, etc.); the secret police had to secretly open people's mail to discover their most intimate opinions, while we trumpet them voluntarily on social media for all to see. So, communist rule might have been crude in its repression, but some of its aspects were actually enforced with more subtlety than what we experience today.

Our contemporary societies have proved remarkably powerless in implementing the critical thinking that should have been solidly anchored after the development of mass democracy for almost a century. We embraced Covid authoritarianism with ease, and we still hear today public calls to monitor and even censor social media,[5] as the latter are accused of promoting hate speech by failing to filter and delete objectionable posts.[6] As a result, various authorities, including the

4 Muriel Blaive, "Surveillance Society: From Communist Czechoslovakia to Contemporary Western Democracies," *East Central Europe* 49, nos. 2–3 (2022): 254–75.

5 See for instance Meg Tirrell, "Social Media Presents 'Profound Risk of Harm' for Kids, Surgeon General Says, Calling Attention to Lack of Research," *CNN*, May 24, 2023, https://edition.cnn.com/2023/05/23/health/social-media-kids-surgeon-general-advisory-wellness/index.html.

6 United Nations, "'Urgent Need' for More Accountability from Social Media Giants to Curb Hate Speech: UN Experts," January 6, 2023, https://news.un.org/en/story/2023/01/1132232.

EU, demand an ever stricter censorship of content by social media and control of social media.[7] As a human rights activist put it, "Coronavirus has started a censorship pandemic: governments around the world are banning fake news about the crisis—and cracking down on their critics while they're at it."[8] But where does criticism end and fake news begin? When has ordinary disagreement become such an outdated notion that it should be outlawed? Why should we either fully agree with people or else ban them? Where has the art of the debate gone? Our "cancel culture" predated Covid,[9] but it has grown significantly worse since.

As my colleague Libora Oates-Indruchová has shown in her masterwork on censorship in late socialism,[10] censorship inevitably leads to what historians of communism call a "social contract," i.e., a form of negotiation between social actors and the authorities to determine what behavior and public speech are acceptable. The regime tries to impose as much censorship as society will tolerate without protesting, while society tries to speak out as much as possible without provoking the regime's ire. While searching for the limits of acceptable canon, social actors resort to self-censorship. Yet, for obvious reasons, self-censorship is the very opposite

7 "Online Platforms Targeted As the EU's Biggest Ever Shake-Up of Digital Rules Kicks in," *Euronews*, August 25, 2023, https://www.euronews.com/my-europe/2023/08/25/online-platforms-targeted-as-the-eus-biggest-ever-shake-up-of-digital-rules-kicks-in.

8 Jacob Mchangama, "Coronavirus Has Started a Censorship Pandemic: Governments around the World Are Banning Fake News about the Crisis—and Cracking down on Their critics While They're at it," *Foreign Policy*, April 1, 2020, https://foreignpolicy.com/2020/04/01/coronavirus-censorship-pandemic-disinformation-fake-news-speech-freedom/.

9 Bret Stephens, "The Dying Art of Disagreement," *The New York Times*, September 24, 2017, https://www.nytimes.com/2017/09/24/opinion/dying-art-of-disagreement.html.

10 Libora Oates-Indruchová, *Censorship in Czech and Hungarian Academic Publishing, 1969-89: Snakes and Ladders* (London: Bloomsbury, 2020).

of progress in science. It leads to the disappearance of critical thinking.[11]

In a situation of heightened scientific uncertainty as was the case with Covid, it was not only politically unacceptable but scientifically extremely damaging to have incited any scientist who might have had productive doubts to remain silent. The notion that censorship is efficient is itself questionable; it doesn't stop the poisoning of the public sphere by hate speech, fake news, or conspiracy theories, which is something even such liberal outlets as the *Guardian* understood before Covid;[12] what censorship is very effective at, on the other hand, is curbing critical perspectives on governmental policies,[13] in other words, at controlling legitimate political opposition. During Covid, it became rapidly obvious that "fighting the pandemic" became a guise for controlling public speech, pointedly in order to determine the best method to fight the virus but opening the door to a much wider control of the public sphere via surveillance and biopolitics.

The historical role of biopolitics in exposing the urge to control and surveil

Biopolitics, i.e., the way in which authorities derive power by controlling the human body, were a concern long before Covid. This research was largely initiated by Michel Foucault

---

11 See Joanna Kempner, "The Chilling Effect: How Do Researchers React to Controversy?" *PLOS Medicine* 6, no. 1 (2009), https://journals.plos.org/plosmedicine/article?id=10.1371/journal.pmed.0050222.

12 See Jon Henley, "Global Crackdown on Fake News Raises Censorship Concerns," *The Guardian*, August 24, 2018, https://www.theguardian.com/media/2018/apr/24/global-crackdown-on-fake-news-raises-censorship-concerns.

13 Peter Noorland, "Artificial Intelligence—Intelligent Politics: Challenges and Opportunities for Media and Democracy," Series "Covid and Free Speech: The Impact of Covid-19 and Ensuing Measures on Freedom of Expression in Council of Europe Member States," Council of Europe, 2020, https://rm.coe.int/covid-and-free-speech-en/1680a03f3a.

in a historical analysis which retraced surveillance culture to Renaissance Europe and the birth of the modern state. Foucault highlighted the direct relationship of the latter to power and disciplinary behavior and its evolution over time, be it via prison, medicine, or sexuality. Post-9/11, discussions on curtailing freedoms for the sake of security and the rise of the biosecurity state intensified, with philosopher Giorgio Agamben critiquing the "state of exception" in the US.[14] Sociologist David Lyon also explored the evolution of surveillance amidst technological advancements and distinguished its detrimental from its beneficial aspects.[15] Julian Assange's WikiLeaks and Edward Snowden's disclosures on electronic surveillance by the NSA revived debates on individual freedom versus institutional surveillance. This shift towards a "surveillance culture," in which surveillance has become integral to everyday life, has raised concerns about its societal impact.[16]

David Lyon notes that Western citizens have not only failed to resist this new surveillance culture, but they engage with it and even initiate it and desire it.[17] This insightful remark regarding the voluntary or semi-voluntary nature of people's compliance became even more pertinent with the normalization of surveillance for health purposes during Covid. It hinted at the way in which surveillance would lead to the self-surveillance of society, i.e., to denunciation, public shaming, and the blaming of "others"—the "irresponsible" people who refrain

14 Giorgio Agamben, *State of Exception* (Chicago: University of Chicago Press, 2005).

15 See David Lyon, *The Electronic Eye: The Rise of Surveillance Society* (Minneapolis: University of Minnesota Press, 2014); David Lyon, *Surveillance Society: Monitoring Everyday Life* (Buckingham: Open University Press, 2001).

16 See Muriel Blaive, "Surveillance Society: From Communist Czechoslovakia to Contemporary Western Democracies," in "Surveillance of Culture, Culture of Surveillance," ed. Muriel Blaive, special issue, *East Central Europe* 49, nos. 2–3 (2022), 254–75.

17 David Lyon, "Surveillance Culture: Engagement, Exposure, and Ethics in Digital Modernity," *International Journal of Communication* 11 (2017): 824–25.

from wearing masks, for instance. The new enemy became not only the virus, which threatened an idealized state of health purity, but the non-compliant humans who might spread it and endanger law-abiding citizens. The pandemic can thus be theorized as the implementation of a new form of puritanism, one which separated the "clean" from the "unclean."[18]

The Swedish model: When science became "anti-science"

The issue of individual and collective survival and how to achieve it was widely debated during Covid. It involved confronting another Agamben concept, the notion of bare life, i.e., of individual survival at all costs, through herd immunity, i.e., the building of collective immunity by letting the least fragile part of society face the virus. The debate was also framed as an alternative between human dignity and utilitarianism,[19] an issue in which Sweden featured prominently since it was the only Western country not to implement blanket lockdowns. The Swedish strategy, defined by its chief epidemiologist Anders Tegnell, who, unlike in other Western countries, is completely independent from the interference of politicians, faced a violent international backlash. The *New York Times*, among others, called Sweden a "pariah state."[20]

---

18 See Zoe Williams, "No Dancing, No Pubs, No Zoos, No Christmas: This Pandemic is Heaven for Puritans," *The Guardian*, October 3, 2020, https://www.theguardian.com/world/2020/oct/03/no-dancing-no-pubs-no-zoos-no-christmas-this-pandemic-is-heaven-for-puritans. See also Madeleine Grant, "Britain Is Stuck in a Priggish World of Covid Puritanism," *The Telegraph*, May 11, 2022, https://www.telegraph.co.uk/opinion/2022/05/11/britain-stuck-priggish-world-covid-puritanism/.

19 See Lapo Lappin, "The Biopolitics of Herd Immunity," in *Sweden's Pandemic Experiment*, ed. Sigurd Bergmann and Martin Lindström (London: Routledge, 2022), 235–55.

20 Thomas Erdbrink, "Sweden Tries Out a New Status: Pariah State," *The New York Times*, July 7, 2020, https://www.nytimes.com/2020/06/22/world/europe/sweden-coronavirus-pariah-scandinavia.html.

Yet, Tegnell did nothing but stick to the pandemic plan he had co-drafted with several authors, including none other than Neil Ferguson, the famous statistician from Imperial College London who so wildly exaggerated the predicted number of deaths from Covid that it led to the British and other lockdowns (see Chapter 3). Their common article stated in 2011 that health officials must weigh the potential benefits of reducing transmission against the socio-medical, ethical, and human cost of lockdown.[21] Tegnell heeded the warning; Ferguson did not.

Today, this raging debate has been cut short by Sweden's undeniable victory since Sweden secured the lowest excess mortality in Europe during the period 2020-2022, according to its own statistics.[22] Less than 7% of the deaths that had been predicted by July 2020 by the Imperial College model materialized.[23] If excess mortality were to be compared to the previous five years before Covid rather than three years, then Norway and Denmark secured a slightly lower rate than Sweden, and Sweden would have the third lowest record.[24] The *Economist* came to the same conclusion via its own

21 Simon Cauchemez, Neil M. Ferguson, Claude Wachtel, Anders Tegnell et al., "Closure of Schools during an Influenza Pandemic," *The Lancet Infectious Diseases*, August 2009, https://www.thelancet.com/journals/laninf/article/PIIS1473-3099(09)70176-8/fulltext.

22 According to Statistics Sweden, see Therese Bergstedt, "Anders Tegnell: gillar inte ordet 'revansch,'" *Svenska Dagbladet*, March 4, 2023, https://www.svd.se/a/JQvVnj/anders-tegnell-efter-pandemin-overdodlighet-ger-inte-hela-svaret. For a solid discussion of the numbers and their context, see also Johan Norberg, "Sweden during the Pandemic: Pariah or Paragon?" Cato Institute, August 29, 2023, https://www.cato.org/policy-analysis/sweden-during-pandemic.

23 Norberg, "Sweden during the Pandemic."

24 Norberg, "Sweden during the Pandemic." See also the statistics of the website Our World in Data, https://ourworldindata.org/explorers/coronavirus-data-explorer?time=2023-01-01&facet=none&country=DNK~SWE~NOR~-DEU~FRA~ITA~ESP~NLD~BEL~CHE~AUT~LUX~GBR~PRT~-FIN~IRL~USA~AUS~NZL&hideControls=true&Metric=Excess+mortality+%28%25%29&Interval=Cumulative&Relative+to+Population=true&Color+by+test+positivity=false.

calculations.[25] Far from resulting in a disaster, the Swedish strategy was a resounding success, especially compared to the countries that criticized it most. Sweden's excess death rate reached 5.6%, compared to 10% in Britain and 14% in the US. According to the *Economist*'s methodology, Sweden's excess death rate reached around 180 per 100,000 people, compared to 345 in Britain and 400 in the United States. "After all was said and done, astonishingly, Sweden had one of the lowest excess death rates of all European countries and less than half that of the United States."[26]

The instrumentalization of fear helps develop a dangerous "digital authoritarianism"

Edward Snowden cautioned in April 2020:

> As authoritarianism spreads, as emergency laws proliferate, as we sacrifice our rights, we also sacrifice our capability to arrest the slide into a less liberal and less free world. Do you truly believe that when the first wave, this second wave, the 16th wave of the coronavirus is a long-forgotten memory, that these capabilities will not be kept? That these datasets will not be kept? No matter how it is being used, what is being built is the architecture of oppression.[27]

Yuval Noah Harari similarly warned about the dangers posed by the Covid regime. In March 2020, he wrote that the choices we made now could change our lives for years to come, so we should choose our measures carefully:

---

25 Norberg, "Sweden during the Pandemic."

26 Norberg, "Sweden during the Pandemic."

27 Trone Dowd, "Snowden Warns Governments Are Using Coronavirus to Build 'the Architecture of Oppression,'" *Vice TV*, April 9, 2020, https://www.vice.com/en/article/bvge5q/snowden-warns-governments-are-using-coronavirus-to-build-the-architecture-of-oppression.

> Many short-term emergency measures will become a fixture of life. That is the nature of emergencies. They fast-forward historical processes. Decisions that in normal times could take years of deliberation are passed in a matter of hours. Immature and even dangerous technologies are pressed into service, because the risks of doing nothing are bigger. Entire countries serve as guinea pigs in large-scale social experiments.[28]

One of the most important choices we faced, he claimed, was between "totalitarian surveillance and citizen empowerment." Modern technology now makes it possible to monitor everyone, all the time. This is why "the epidemic might ... mark an important watershed in the history of surveillance."[29] Surveillance can always be justified as a temporary measure which will go away when the emergency is over, but "temporary measures have a nasty habit of outlasting emergencies, especially as there is always a new emergency lurking on the horizon."[30]

Amnesty International later expressed the same concern, noting in 2021 that freedom of expression was globally under attack in the context of the Covid pandemic: "Governments have used the pandemic as a pretext to muzzle critical voices. Amnesty International is concerned that Covid-19 related restrictions are not just temporary measures but are part of an ongoing onslaught on human rights and civic space."[31]

Haaretz, a quality liberal newspaper attuned to military conditions since Israel is frequently at war, has keenly

---

28 Yuval Noah Harari, "The World after Coronavirus—The Storm Will Pass. But the Choices We Make Now Could Change Our Lives for Years to Come," *Financial Times*, March 20, 2020, https://www.ft.com/content/19d90308-6858-11ea-a3c9-1fe6fedcca75.

29 Harari, "The World after Coronavirus."

30 Harari, "The World after Coronavirus."

31 Amnesty International, "Silenced and Misinformed: Freedom of Expression in Danger During Covid-19," 2021, https://www.amnesty.org/en/documents/pol30/4751/2021/en/.

documented the militarization of the Covid crisis.[32] It established a parallel between the Covid security-oriented approach and the generals and military commentators generally heard in wartime, noting that health experts and former hospital directors are also men from the heart of the Israeli establishment.[33] Shin Bet, the internal security service, implemented extraordinary means of surveillance, an "invasion of privacy" under the pretext of the Covid response, which was little criticized "despite the fact that the extreme measures were approved in the middle of the night without parliamentary oversight, while the courts were paralyzed and the citizens were in their homes."[34] The Israeli "Big coronavirus brother" was left free to track where Israelis were and what they were doing.[35]

Worse, the more radical members of the government, including Naftali Bennett, used this public and media silence to exacerbate the Israeli government's "attack on human rights." Bennett brought in a dubious cybersecurity firm, the NSO Group,[36] with which he might, according to *Haaretz*,

---

32 Edan Ring, "The Militarization of the Coronavirus Crisis, As Seen on Israeli TV," *Haaretz*, April 12, 2020, https://www.haaretz.com/opinion/2020-04-12/ty-article-opinion/.premium/the-militarization-of-the-coronavirus-crisis-as-seen-on-israeli-tv/0000017f-e47f-d7b2-a77f-e77f0d9a0000.

33 Ring, "The Militarization of the Coronavirus Crisis."

34 Ring, "The Militarization of the Coronavirus Crisis."

35 Rafaella Goichmann, "Shin Bet Tracking, Police Check-Ups: Pandemic Spurs Rise of Israel's Big Coronavirus Brother," *Haaretz*, April 9, 2020, https://www.haaretz.com/israel-news/2020-04-09/ty-article/.premium/coronavirus-pandemic-spurs-rise-of-a-big-doctor-state-in-israel/0000017f-e22b-d804-ad7f-f3fb24420000.

36 See Rafaella Goichmann, "Israeli Defense Ministry Teaming Up with Spyware Firm NSO to Fight Coronavirus," *Haaretz*, March 29, 2020, https://www.haaretz.com/israel-news/2020-03-29/ty-article/.premium/israeli-defense-chief-plans-to-employ-spyware-firm-nso-in-fight-against-coronavirus/0000017f-db5f-d856-a37f-ffdf06810000. To get a better idea of NSO Group's practices and bring more context around the Covid suppression of speech, see the documentary film from Anne Poiret and Arthur Bouvard, "Global Spyware Scandal: Exposing Pegasus" (two parts), *PBS Frontline*, January 3, and January 10, 2023, https://www.pbs.org/wgbh/frontline/documentary/global-spywa-

have personal ties, with the argument that "in war, there are no tenders."[37] *Haaretz* columnist Edan Ring noted: "Public and media cooperation with the security-oriented perception of the crisis gives the politicians a green light to do things that would be unimaginable in ordinary times and constitutes a dangerous precedent from which it will be impossible to retreat."[38]

Giorgio Agamben counted amongst the earliest critics of Covid measures, too. He blasted on his personal blog the "frantic, irrational, and absolutely unwarranted emergency measures adopted for a supposed epidemic of coronavirus" and the way in which the "media and the authorities do their utmost to create a climate of panic, thus provoking a true state of exception, with severe limitations on movement and the suspension of daily life and work activities for entire regions."[39] He noted that the state of exception was increasingly used as a normal governing paradigm and that the "invention of an epidemic" could easily replace terrorism as a justification for exceptional measures. The "state of fear" called for a "state of collective panic," so that "in a perverse vicious circle, the limitation of freedom imposed by governments is accepted in the name of a desire for safety, which has been created by the same governments who now intervene to satisfy it.[40]

---

re-scandal-exposing-pegasus/. The film was originally broadcast in French for ARTE France, but the English-speaking, PBS version of the film is available on Amazon Prime Video and also on YouTube, at https://www.youtube.com/watch?v=7EF1nITrdKs (part 1) and https://www.youtube.com/watch?v=LK-FLVKBJdYw (part 2.)

37 Ring, "The Militarization of the Coronavirus Crisis."

38 Ring, "The Militarization of the Coronavirus Crisis."

39 Giorgio Agamben, "The State of Exception Provoked by an Unmotivated Emergency," *Positions Politics*, February 26, 2022, https://positionspolitics.org/giorgio-agamben-the-state-of-exception-provoked-by-an-unmotivated-emergency/.

40 Agamben, "The State of Exception."

Despite the quality of Agamben's biopolitical analysis, what pundits really reacted to was the formulation "supposed epidemic of coronavirus." One of his English translators denounced him as a paranoid who sounded "disturbingly like a right-wing crank" and influenced "very far-right politicians" and "online anti-vaxxers,"[41] while paying little or no heed to his perceptive warning about the way in which the security state would indeed use the pandemic as a pretext to expand and consolidate. As mentioned above, anyone stepping out of the official narrative was almost automatically designated as a far right or alt-right supporter, and Agamben was no exception—which was as ironical as it was absurd for a self-designated left-wing anarchist. Again, the parallel with the communist regimes, in which any critic was labeled a fascist or fascist sympathizer, cannot but come to mind.

Agamben also posted on his blog "Biosecurity and Politics" that state security was using health as a pretext for its strategy. He claimed that "at issue is nothing less than the creation of a sort of 'health terror'" involving a scenario in which data is presented as "extreme," the "logic of the worst" as a "regime of political rationality," and the production of a "good citizenship" as one in which "imposed obligations are presented as evidence of altruism" and in which the citizen becomes "juridically obliged to health (biosecurity)."[42]

Other scholars of biopolitics and/or journalists concur about this biopolitical risk. The 2020 documentary film by Sylvain Louvet shown on ARTE, *Seven Billion Suspects: The Totalitarian*

41 See, for instance, Adam Kotsko, "What Happened to Giorgio Agamben?" *Slate*, February 20, 2020, https://slate.com/human-interest/2022/02/giorgio-agamben-covid-holocaust-comparison-right-wing-protest.html.

42 Thanks to D. Alan Dean, an English translation of Agamben's blog post can be found here: https://d-dean.medium.com/biosecurity-and-politics-giorgio-agamben-396f9ab3b6f4. See also his volume *Where Are We Now? The Epidemic as Politics* (London: Eris, 2021).

Society, for instance, "draws up a global panorama of the security obsession, with one chilling observation: digital totalitarianism is for tomorrow."[43] Or rather, this "tomorrow" became "today" under Covid; as the pandemic unfolded, Louvet warned about the proliferation of technological surveillance in the name of "security," which was increasingly detrimental to our freedoms.[44] He expressed his worry that this new "market of fear" would be used to "garner acceptance."[45] As the film title suggests, every one of us is now a suspect—what the "crime" is supposed to be can be easily readjusted on a day-to-day basis. The irony is that his film was made in 2019 and first broadcast in April 2020, but it would most likely never have been shown on TV had it been made during or after Covid, as it would doubtless have been interpreted as a criticism of official pandemic policies.

Totalitarianism, authoritarianism, and democracy with a totalitarian intent

The unparalleled level of societal compliance, occasionally bordering on fanaticism, which could be observed during Covid brought Western societies closer to the dystopian world of George Orwell's *Nineteen Eighty-Four*. This is what led to the popularity of Mattias Desmet, a professor of clinical psychology, who noted already before Covid that the emergence of

43 See Sylvain Louvet, *Tous surveillés: sept milliards de suspects*, ARTE, 2019, https://www.imdb.com/title/tt12182636/?ref_=tt_pg. This film can be watched for free in French with English subtitles on the webpage of Radio France Internationale, https://www.rfi.fr/en/video/20201206-7-billion-suspects-the-surveillance-society.

44 Olivier Tesquet, "'Tous surveillés' sur ARTE: 'Attention à cette société du tout-sécuritaire qui se dessine!,'" *Télérama*, April 21, 2020, https://www.telerama.fr/television/tous-surveilles-sur-arte-attention-a-cette-societe-du-tout-securitaire-qui-se-dessine,n6628012.php.

45 Tesquet, "'Tous surveillés' sur ARTE."

woke culture was giving "rise to the call for a new, hyper-strict government that emerged from within the population itself."[46]

The difference with the past, he writes, is that this dystopian "new totalitarianism" is "no longer led by flamboyant 'mob leaders' such as Josef Stalin or Adolf Hitler but by dull bureaucrats and technocrats."[47] Desmet proposes to analyze this through the psychological phenomenon of mass formation, a process which renders possible the "shocking behaviors of a 'totalitarized' population, including an exaggerated willingness of individuals to sacrifice their own personal interests out of solidarity with the collective (i.e., the masses), a profound intolerance of dissident voices, and a pronounced susceptibility to pseudo-scientific indoctrination and propaganda."[48]

But historians of Nazism and communism, myself included, have spent the last forty years dispelling this simplistic view of a "totalitarized" population, restituting agency to individual social actors instead. The concept of totalitarianism originally seemed to make sense to describe Stalinism and Nazism insofar as it helped in understanding how individuals could support inhumane and degrading policies. But the concept also served to wash out populations of guilt: if the "totalitarian system" was guilty, no one was concretely responsible anymore. On such a theoretical basis, it becomes difficult to account for the partial support of society for such regimes. Without denying the genuine and sometimes horrific suffering stemming from living under a dictatorship, the totalitarian aspiration of any regime is contradicted in practice by the complexity of everyday life and the involvement of every citizen in the maintenance of the regime by micro-compromises on an

46 Mattias Desmet, *The Psychology of Totalitarianism* (London: Chelsea Green, 2022), 7.

47 Desmet, *The Psychology of Totalitarianism*, 7.

48 Desmet, *The Psychology of Totalitarianism*, 8.

everyday basis. In the case of communism, Václav Havel called this "auto-totalitarianism." Sociologist Michel Maffesoli calls it "soft totalitarianism," including in the Covid case, one in which incoherent orders issued by the technostructure are disconnected from the popular masses while fear is staged.[49]

Desmet claims that up to a third of the population might be mesmerized and become insusceptible to logic or rational arguments.[50] But this is not supported by socio-political history. There is a significant difference between *appearing* subdued and simply waiting for the moment when it is safe to speak freely again. Accurately gauging the true level of support for a regime (the Putin or Hamas regimes come to mind today) is almost impossible until that regime collapses and a free public sphere is restored. This is yet another reason why the censorship imposed on critics of the Covid response was so unfortunate: by silencing dissent, it obscured the evolving measure of public support on the matter.[51] As a social historian, I would not be surprised if, in the future, the Covid response was found to have been, in fact, partly or largely unpopular at the societal level depending on the time period.

Where Desmet tends to see the populations as "hypnotized" and unable to "think critically,"[52] he supposes, on the contrary, in the far-right Gustave Le Bon tradition, that only elites can restore "consciousness" and "sanity."[53] But I would

---

49 See Michel Maffesoli, *L'ère des soulèvements: Emeutes et confinements—Les derniers soubresauts de la modernité* (Paris: Le Cerf, 2021).

50 Desmet, *The Psychology of Totalitarianism*, 8.

51 If we are to bring the masses into the equation, then this analysis of mass psychosis and how it led to a "precautionary principle" which paralyzed political action is more useful: René Girard and Jean-Loup Bonnamy, *Quand la psychose fait dérailler le monde* (Paris: Gallimard–Tracts, 2020).

52 Desmet, *The Psychology of Totalitarianism*, 8.

53 See the analysis by Thierry Simonelli, "The Strange Epidemic of 'Mass Formation Analysis': A Critical Reading of the Book 'The Psychology of Totalitarianism' by Mattias Desmet," *Thierry Simonelli* (blog), August 22, 2022, https://www.thsimonelli.net/the-strange-epidemic-of-mass-formation-hypnosis/. Many thanks to Éloïse Adde for this reference.

contend in the case of the Covid response that the opposite was true: it was in large part the elites who appeared "hypnotized" and unable to "think critically," while ordinary people expressed a stronger critical mind, consciousness, and sanity. The fact that elites monopolize public discourse does not mean that they are representative of society; it only shows that they occupy the microphone.

So with Covid, we have for the first time in modern history experienced something I call democracy with a totalitarian intent. We are doubtless still living in democracies, but authorities in almost all Western countries introduced measures which very much resembled the censorship, surveillance, and propaganda of the communist model, albeit packaged in a more acceptable form. The fear of the virus was, in particular, aroused and weaponized thanks to a less coercive but perhaps even more manipulative technique than propaganda: nudging. Nudging ensured the compliance of the population thanks to covert persuasion and peer pressure via emotion; as a result, the level of surveillance and denunciations exerted by society upon itself reached new heights.

Nudging: A frightening technique used to elicit social behavior

The behavioral science intervention known as "nudging" is a psychological method of persuasion meant to "often operate below people's conscious awareness" and "frequently relies on inflating emotional discomfort to change behavior." In the case of Covid, nudging served the "state's often-covert deployment of fear inflation, guilt/shame, and peer pressure/scapegoating to strengthen the Covid communications strategy."[54]

54 Gary Sidley, "UK Government Use of Behavioral Science Strategies in Covid-Event Messaging: Responsibility and Communication Ethics in Times of 'Crisis,'"

Journalist Laura Dodsworth unearthed a report of the Scientific Pandemic Influenza Group on Behavior (SPI-B) from March 22, 2020, which lamented that the British population was not sufficiently frightened by Covid and recommended in its report *Options for Increasing Adherence to Social Distancing Measures* a chilling mixture of incentives and coercion. This guide makes an inventory of techniques to lead the population to act in the desired way: increase the perceived threat, appeal for responsibility to others, positive messaging around actions, tailoring, incentivization, compulsion, and social disapproval. In other words, it describes how to create the modern democracy with totalitarian intent I invoked above, what it called "converting the complacent" by using "hard-hitting emotional messaging," which "needs to emphasize the duty to protect others."[55]

At other times, the messaging should be more positive and framed in terms of protecting oneself and the community: "Some people will be more persuaded by appeals to play by the rules, some by duty to the community, and some to personal risk. All these different approaches are needed."[56] The importance of peer pressure is also discussed, both as social approval and social disapproval from one's community. Social approval can be a "powerful source of reward." This can be "provided directly by highlighting examples of good practice and providing strong social encouragement and approval in communications";

AHPb Magazine for Self & Society, 11 (2023-24): 1–21, https://ahpb.org/index.php/gary-sidley-article/?doing_wp_cron=1712218536.8968319892883300781250.

55 SAGE behavioral science sub-group SPI-B, "Options for Increasing Adherence to Social Distancing Measures," *gov.uk*, March 22, 2020, https://assets.publishing.service.gov.uk/media/5ecd084586650c76acac37e0/25-options-for-increasing-adherence-to-social-distancing-measures-22032020.pdf, 1–2. Cited by Laura Dodsworth, *A State of Fear: How the UK Government Weaponized Fear During the Covid-19 Pandemic* (London: Pinter & Martin, 2021), 2.

56 SPI-B, "Options for Increasing Adherence," 2.

moreover, members of the community could be encouraged to provide it to each other. This could have a "beneficial spill-over effect of promoting social cohesion."[57]

As for "social disapproval," it was deemed capable of "preventing anti-social behavior or discouraging failure to enact pro-social behavior." However, the report warned, the engagement of social disapproval needed to be "carefully managed to avoid victimization, scapegoating, and misdirected criticism." It also needed to be accompanied by "clear messaging and promotion of strong collective identity."[58] This latter warning went rather unheeded.

Such an experiment in social engineering of mass coercion was looked upon with optimism:

> Experience with UK enforcement legislation such as compulsory seat belt use suggests that, with adequate preparation, rapid change can be achieved. Some other countries have introduced mandatory self-isolation on a wide scale without evidence of major public unrest and a large majority of the UK's population appear to be supportive of more coercive measures.[59]

Some aspects of this mental manipulation are chilling. In Los Angeles, for instance, children were made to "apologize to their dying elders for spreading Covid-19."[60] Can we wonder that the mental health of children and the youth took such a toll during the pandemic when they were made to feel guilty

---

57 SPI-B, "Options for Increasing Adherence," 2.
58 SPI-B, "Options for Increasing Adherence," 2.
59 SPI-B, "Options for Increasing Adherence," 2.
60 Rong-Gong Lin II and Luke Money, "Children Apologize to Their Dying Elders for Spreading COVID-19 As L.A. County Reels," *Los Angeles Times*, January 12, 2021, https://www.latimes.com/california/story/2021-01-12/children-apologizing-to-parents-grandparents-spreading-coronavirus-into-families-as-l-a-county-reels.

if they ever flouted the "Stay home, stay safe" message, or its equivalents in other countries?[61] The consequences of the pandemic response will still be felt for many years to come.

Summary of Chapter 1

Chapter 1 laid the groundwork for understanding "digital authoritarianism" through the lens of social compliance and the normalization of fear. Drawing on historical lessons from communist regimes, it emphasized the pivotal role of controlling information to maintain authoritarian rule. The Covid pandemic served as a revealing stress test for democracy, exposing the ease with which authoritarian measures were embraced. Nudging, by channeling societal behavior, contributed to widespread compliance and to a lack of critical thinking. By dissecting this surveillance culture, the chapter underscored the emergence of a new form of political organization: democracy with a totalitarian intent.

61 Ashley Abramson, "Children's Mental Health Is in Crisis," *American Psychological Association* 53, no. 1 (2022): 69, https://www.apa.org/monitor/2022/01/special-childrens-mental-health.

Chapter 2

Collateral damage, censorship, and hubris: The practical reality of the lockdown

> ... from the moral point of view, pain cannot be outweighed by pleasure, and especially not one man's pain by another man's pleasure. Instead of the greatest happiness for the greatest number, one should demand, more modestly, the least amount of avoidable suffering for all; and further, that unavoidable suffering—such as hunger in times of an unavoidable shortage of food—should be distributed as equally as possible.
>
> Karl Popper, *The Open Society and Its Enemies*

Many Westerners, including authorities, panicked during the Covid epidemic. But this authentic distress was accompanied by a remarkable level of disregard for the ordeal experienced in the developing world as a result of Western and local lockdowns. Medical anthropologist Carlo Caduff speaks of a "neoliberal pandemic,"[1] which has resulted in neoliberal policies that have defunded healthcare but also ingrained the belief that citizens are responsible for their own protection and for the protection of others. This has served to promote a "political economy of free carelessness" while obscuring democratic accountability.[2]

1 Yarimar Bonilla, "Covid, Twitter, and Critique: An Interview with Carlo Caduff," *American Anthropologist*, May 25, 2020, https://www.americananthropologist.org/online-content/covid-twitter-and-critique-an-interview-with-carlo-caduff.

2 Bonilla, "Covid, Twitter, and Critique."

The poor in developing countries were free to die as long as we in the West survived

In March 2020, we ignored the human disaster that our lockdowns unleashed outside of the Western world as humanitarian aid faced "the first world crisis ... of the precautionary principle."[3] Angered by what he saw as the abandonment of vulnerable populations in the developing world, Pierre Brunet spoke of "a form of dictatorship of political thought, of globalized governance ... (we no longer tolerate the very idea of death, as if we had acquired a kind of enforceable right before the state not to die.)" This right "not to die" was only enforced in Western states, however; the author predicted on the contrary that the number of people suffering from hunger in the world would rise from 135 million in 2019 to 265 million in 2020.[4]

People did die in Africa because food and medicines were not delivered,[5] while the only planes in the air were delivering face masks to Westerners. People died of hunger on the Indian subcontinent[6] because they lost their jobs due to the collapse of Western industrial consumption and due to their own stringent lockdowns.[7] Mothers in labor died in Uganda due to

---

3 Pierre Brunet, "L'humanitaire à l'épreuve de la peur, ou comment faire face à la première crise mondiale ... du principe de précaution," *Défis humanitaires*, May 12, 2020, https://defishumanitaires.com/2020/05/12/lhumanitaire-a-lepreuve-de-la-peur-ou-comment-faire-face-a-la-premiere-crise-mondiale-du-principe-de-precaution/. On the collateral damage of the lockdown both in the West and in the developing world, see the volume Daniel Briggs, Luke Telford, Anthony Lloyd, Anthony Ellis, and Justin Kotzé, *Lockdown: Social Harm in the Covid-19 Era* (London: Palgrave Macmillan, 2021).

4 Brunet, "L'humanitaire à l'épreuve de la peur."

5 See, for instance, "Coronavirus-Linked Malnutrition Is Killing 10,000 More Children a Month, UN Warns," *France 24*, July 28, 2020, https://www.france24.com/en/20200728-coronavirus-linked-hunger-kills-10-000-children-per-month-says-un.

6 "Covid-19 Disruptions Killed 228,000 Children in South Asia, Says UN Report," *BBC*, March 17, 2021, https://www.bbc.com/news/world-asia-56425115.

7 Jeevant Rampal, "The Hunger Challenge of the Lockdown," *BusinessLine*, May 1, 2020, https://www.thehindubusinessline.com/opinion/the-hunger-challenge-of-the-lockdown/article31480844.ece.

coronavirus lockdowns.[8] How many people will have perished in total? The figures are not yet known but are expected to be in the tens of millions.[9] Yet, Western mainstream media have not been interested in investigating the lockdown and other Covid restrictions as purveyors of death; instead, they almost unfailingly blame "the pandemic."

A research paper of the World Bank from May 2021 showed that up to "1.76 children's lives could potentially be lost due to the economic contraction per Covid-19 fatality averted,"[10] a trade-off which was evidently not in favor of lockdowns. In lower income countries, to remain in lockdown meant to starve, while to feed one's family amounted to breaking the quarantine and risking repression.[11] The lockdown gravely impacted not only food security but the economy, education, hospitality, tourism, leisure, gender relations, domestic violence, domestic abuse, and mental health.[12] A documentary film, *The Children of Nowhere*, shows that hundreds of millions of children in India saw their education devastated—indeed, schools closed for almost two years, but only 8% of rural children were able to attend online classes, and 37% did not

8 Elias Byriabarema, "In Uganda, Mothers in Labor Die amidst Coronavirus Lockdown," *Reuters*, April 9, 2020, https://sg.news.yahoo.com/uganda-mothers-labour-die-amidst-153850240.html.

9 Michaela C. Schippers, "For the Greater Good? The Devastating Ripple Effects of the Covid-19 Crisis," *Frontiers in Psychology*, September 29, 2020, https://www.ncbi.nlm.nih.gov/pmc/articles/PMC7550468//.

10 Lin Ma et.al, "The Intergenerational Mortality Trade-Off of Covid-19 Lockdown Policies," *World Bank Development Research Group*, May 2021, abstract, https://documents1.worldbank.org/curated/en/990621622121589737/pdf/The-Intergenerational-Mortality-Tradeoff-of-COVID-19-Lockdown-Policies.pdf.

11 Kelsey Piper, "The Devastating Consequences of Coronavirus Lockdowns in Poor Countries," *Vox*, April 18, 2020, https://www.vox.com/future-perfect/2020/4/18/21212688/coronavirus-lockdowns-developing-world.

12 See Helen Onyeaka, Christian Anumudu, and Paul Mbaegbu, "Covid-19 Pandemic: A Review of the Global Lockdown and Its Far-Reaching Effects," *Science Progress*, June 1, 2021, https://journals.sagepub.com/doi/10.1177/00368504211019854.

attend any class at all.[13] Also, cases of teenage pregnancies and child marriages soared. A devastation also occurred in Honduras and, again, in Uganda, where millions of children simply never returned to school when it resumed after the lockdown (20% of them in the latter case). In Latin America, young women's sexual and reproductive health went back to what it was decades ago. In Angola, South Africa, Nigeria, Kenya, and many other countries, the impact of school closures, especially on girls, was no less than disastrous.[14]

New Zealand boasted about its success in the pandemic, but this success was predicated on "Covid nationalism," i.e., on tightly closing its borders in a modern form of "apartheid," and on "not appearing to care" about the impact this policy would have on poorer countries dependent on trade.[15] The overall result of this policy and similar ones was dire:

> Middle-income countries saw a dramatic rise of soup kitchens in poor areas as their ability to earn money vanished overnight. Children in poor countries were suddenly unable to access education, and the impact was so severe that on some estimates the follow-through in terms of lost skills will be felt for a century. Death rates in countries like Angola for malaria and dengue fever went through the roof as the state, plunged into an economic crisis more severe than anything since independence, withdrew services. Domestic abuse soared all over the world, while child marriage and trafficking increased.[16]

Policymakers knew exactly what to expect: UNESCO had released a report on March 19, 2020, to lay out that school closures

---

13 Abeer Khan and Kunal Purohit, "The Children of Nowhere," *Collateral Global*, March 23, 2023, https://collateralglobal.org/article/the-children-of-nowhere/.

14 Khan and Purohit, "The Children of Nowhere." See also Caduff, "What Went Wrong."

15 Toby Green and Thomas Fazi, *The Covid Consensus: The Global Assault on Democracy and the Poor—A Critique from the Left* (London: Hurst, 2023), 436–37.

16 Green and Fazi, *The Covid Consensus*, 437.

would mostly affect those who were already underprivileged. They could "only immensely exacerbate inequalities owing to gaps in care caused by the stress and competing responsibilities provoked by this policy."[17] Authorities proceeded with them anyway and got the expected results:

> ...lockdowns were catastrophic. The disruption to economies and education entrenched and deepened inequality and massively expanded national debt, worsening the debt crisis facing the [African] continent.... In 2020 and 2021, Western countries raised interest rates to manage the economic effect of the pandemic. This curtailed the ability of African countries to finance and repay their debt arrangements and has resulted in ballooning interest rates and weakening local currencies.[18]

Already by October 2020, the World Bank estimated that 100 million people had been thrown into extreme poverty; "decades of progress" had "gone into reverse" in the "worst setback" in a generation.[19]

The Western left has become indifferent to inequality

"Lockdowns," wrote Martin Kulldorff on Twitter on January 28, 2021, "have protected the laptop class of young low-risk journalists, scientists, teachers, politicians, and lawyers, while throwing children, the working class, and high-risk older people

---

17 Khan and Purohit, "The Children of Nowhere."

18 Anjuli Webster, "Pandemic Preparations Are Unhealthy," *Mail & Guardian*, March 22, 2024, https://mg.co.za/thought-leader/opinion/2024-03-22-pandemic-preparations-are-unhealthy/.

19 Josh Zumbrun, "Coronavirus Has Thrown around 100 Million People into Extreme Poverty, World Bank Estimates," *Wall Street Journal*, October 7, 2020, https://www.wsj.com/articles/coronavirus-has-thrown-around-100-million-people-into-extreme-poverty-world-bank-estimates-11602086400.

under the bus."[20] The collective reaction of indifference on the part of the academic liberal left has been all the more puzzling that the latter belong to a social class which is typically critical of authoritarianism and which likes to portray itself as attuned to the plight of the poor and disadvantaged. Yet, it attacked those who defended the poor as Covid unfolded:

> Four years ago, a professor of epidemiology, Oxford's Sunetra Gupta, released a study suggesting that Covid may have started to spread earlier than anyone thought, and that as a result of this, the doomsday scenario which some scientists were predicting might not come to pass. The abuse she faced as a result of not yielding to the general hysteria was instructive. It revealed an intellectual establishment where to challenge authority was seen as heresy. Academics who did question the government's strategy ended up having their reputations attacked and their livelihoods threatened. Universities offered no support to dissenters, but stayed silent.[21]

Toby Green and Thomas Fazi asked why the Western "public performance of empathy" and "performative compliance with lockdown measures"[22] was also (and perhaps mainly) practiced by politicians and writers from the left while they "produced ... radical harms for poor people."[23] Indeed, the reactions to the pandemic seem to have gone against all left-wing values. Toby Green even describes the Covid pandemic response on the continent as "neocolonial": "It suppressed indigenous medical systems, disregarded the perspectives of public health officials

20 See Martin Kulldorff (@MartinKulldorff), "Lockdowns have protected the laptop class of young low-risk journalists, scientists, teachers, politicians and lawyers," Twitter, January 28, 2021, 2:20 pm, https://twitter.com/MartinKulldorff/status/1354781489150504962.

21 "Covid and the Politics of Panic," *The Spectator*, March 30, 2024, https://www.spectator.co.uk/article/covid-and-the-politics-of-panic-2/.

22 Green and Fazi, *The Covid Consensus*, 4.

23 Green and Fazi, *The Covid Consensus*, 3.

in Africa, and frontlined Covid vaccinations at the expense of treating other serious medical conditions such as malaria and tuberculosis. On the other hand, the pandemic produced a new billionaire almost every day, inflating inequality across the globe."[24] This policy was not only neocolonial but frankly racist.[25] Carlo Caduff showed that the notion of "global threat" posed by the virus conjured a response framed as requiring "everyone's sacrifice," but that this image "relied on a false assumption of equality." The notion of solidarity proved meaningless in view of the fact that the lockdowns affected people in different ways. It is in fact the most vulnerable who were the most affected by the lockdown.[26]

Oxfam International indeed warned in 2022 that the pandemic was creating one new billionaire every 30 hours, while one million people could be falling into poverty at the same rate.[27] By 2022, the ten richest men had already doubled their fortunes thanks to the pandemic, while the income of 99% of the world population had fallen.[28] The American left, obsessed with and entirely mobilized around the construction of its anti-Trump image, failed to express any indignation or concern or to even collectively engage, as mentioned above, in any critical approach to the Covid response. It displayed the same indifference concerning the lack of access to vaccines among the poorer countries. Millions of Westerners,

---

24 Webster, "Pandemic Preparations."

25 See Bhattacharya, Green, and Oduor, "Is the New WHO Treaty Neo-Colonialism."

26 See Caduff, "What Went Wrong."

27 Annie Thériault and Belinda Torres-Leclerq, "Pandemic Creates New Billionaire Every 30 Hours—Now a Million People Could Fall into Extreme Poverty at Same Rate in 2022," *Oxfam International*, May 23, 2022, https://www.oxfam.org/en/press-releases/pandemic-creates-new-billionaire-every-30-hours-now-million-people-could-fall.

28 Annie Thériault and Belinda Torres-Leclerq, "Ten Richest Men Double Their Fortunes in Pandemic While Incomes of 99 Percent of Humanity Fall," *Oxfam International*, January 17, 2022, https://www.oxfam.org/en/press-releases/ten-richest-men-double-their-fortunes-pandemic-while-incomes-99-percent-humanity.

including many in academia, posed for the camera while getting their vaccine, keen on providing a "good example" to the world but failing to consider how offensive such a display was for those who had no chance of getting it.

Shortsightedness drastically limited rational discourse. On the one hand, the trio Donald Trump-Jair Bolsonaro-Boris Johnson downplayed the dangers of Covid. Worse, they politicized the issue, as populist politicians typically do: insofar as everything is about them, anyone criticizing their Covid denial was pitched as their enemy, the "leftist." Alas, the liberal left around the globe fell right into this trap; as if in a mirror, anyone criticizing stringent Covid policies was automatically associated with the "populist" enemy and had to be silenced. This attitude greatly contributed to hiding the disaster caused by the lockdowns also in the West.

The collateral damage of the lockdowns has also been devastating in the West

Lockdowns have proved useless against Covid: "Whatever we did, the virus just kept on spreading: this is a fair summary of what happened in 2020."[29] On the other hand, the lockdowns are now known to have caused considerable damage in the West as well,[30] costing, for instance, as of February 2024, 111,000 years of lives in Europe to skin cancer patients alone due to delayed diagnoses.[31] In a study published in March 2024 on the server of the *Wall Street Journal* rather

29 See Green and Fazi, *The Covid Consensus*, 436.

30 See Ross Clark, "Did Lockdowns Cause More Harm Than Good?" *The Spectator*, February 18, 2024, https://www.spectator.co.uk/article/did-lockdowns-cause-more-harm-than-good/.

31 Lara V. Maul, Dagmar Jamiolkowski, Rebecca A. Lapides et al., "Health Economic Consequences Associated with Covid-19-Related Delay in Melanoma Diagnosis in Europe," *JAMA Network Open*, February 16, 2024, https://jamanetwork.com/journals/jamanetworkopen/fullarticle/2815226.

than in an academic journal (although it appears adequately sourced), perhaps because one of its lead authors, Scott Atlas, was pushed to resign from his position at Stanford due to its critical stance on Covid lockdowns,[32] it was estimated that the deaths caused by the lockdowns and societal disruptions in the US since 2020 were "likely around 400,000, as much as 100 times the number of Covid deaths the lockdowns prevented." As mentioned earlier, the report quotes a study published in the Proceedings of the National Academy of Sciences, which found that the US "would have had 1.60 million fewer deaths if it had had the performance of Sweden."[33]

On a side note, the lead author of this study, John Ioannidis from Stanford, was censored on YouTube for claiming in a 2021 documentary film that the national reaction to Covid was the result of sensationalism and of a state of panic. The *Washington Post* claimed that he was "losing the argument," while his critics said he violated his "own principles of intellectual rigor," "refusing to admit his mistaken judgements and recklessly lending a scientific imprimatur to forces that defy public-health directives for irrational reasons."[34] These accusations, proffered in December 2020, have not aged well. Ioannidis' analyses, on the other hand, are more salient than ever.

Amidst the staggering costs of lockdowns, Scott Atlas's study from March 2024 quotes the fact that in spring 2020, nearly half of the US's 650,000 chemotherapy patients did not

32 For an example of the coverage he received from mainstream media, see Philip Bump, "Scott Atlas Will Forever Be the Face of Surrender to the Coronavirus," *The Washington Post*, December 1, 2020, https://www.washingtonpost.com/politics/2020/12/01/scott-atlas-will-forever-be-face-surrender-coronavirus/.

33 John P. A. Ioannidis, Francesco Zonta, and Michael Levitt, "Variability in Excess Deaths across Countries with Different Vulnerability during 2020-2023," *PNAS*, November 29, 2023, https://www.pnas.org/doi/full/10.1073/pnas.2309557120.

34 Peter Jamison, "A Top Scientist Questioned Virus Lockdowns on Fox News. The Backlash Was Fierce," *The Washington Post*, December 16, 2020, https://www.washingtonpost.com/dc-md-va/2020/12/16/john-ioannidis-coronavirus-lockdowns-fox-news/.

get treatment, and 85% of living organ transplants weren't completed. Moreover:

> According to the Bureau of Labor Statistics, as many as 49 million Americans were out of work in May 2020. This shock had health consequences. A National Bureau of Economic Research study found that the lockdown unemployment shock is projected to result in 840,000 to 1.22 million excess deaths over the next 15 to 20 years, disproportionately killing women and minorities. By one estimate today's children will lose $17 trillion in lifetime earnings owing to school closings. They may also suffer shorter life expectancy, which is linked to income and educational attainment.[35]

Indeed, the lockdowns caused considerable damage to Western children. School closures are now known not to have significantly slowed down the spread of the Covid virus, but on the other hand they caused what will possibly be irreparable harm to the impacted generations; they caused long-term academic decline, especially in poor communities, as well as a considerable rise in anxiety and mental health issues among the youth.[36] Babies and young children also suffered developmental setbacks.[37] Perhaps lockdowns did save lives, the *Spectator*

---

35 Scott Atlas, Steve H. Hanke, Philip G. Kerpen, and Casey B. Mulligan, *COVID Lessons Learned: A Retrospective after Four Years*, Committee to Unleash Prosperity, March 2024, https://committeetounleashprosperity.com/wpcontent/uploads/2024/03/240313_CTUP_COVIDCommitteeReport_Doc.pdf, 10.

36 Sarah Mervosh, Claire Cain Miller, and Francesca Paris, "What the Data Says about Pandemic School Closures, Four Years Later," *The New York Times*, March 18, 2024, https://www.nytimes.com/2024/03/18/upshot/pandemic-school-closures-data.html. See also my tweet on this article: Muriel Blaive (@MurielBlaivePhD), "After slandering for four years the people who tried to warn about the disastrous effect school closures would have on education," Twitter, March 18, 2024, 3:00 pm, https://twitter.com/MurielBlaivePhD/status/1769725569040547987; as well as Hannah Fearn, "How Covid Lockdowns Hit Mental Health of Teenage Boys Hardest," *The Guardian*, March 23, 2024, https://www.theguardian.com/society/2024/mar/23/how-covid-lockdowns-hit-mental-health-of-teenage-boys-hardest.

37 Hannah Devlin, "Young and Old: How the Covid Pandemic Has Affected Every UK Generation," *The Guardian*, March 21, 2024, https://www.theguardian.

mused, "but for how long, given that most of those who did succumb to Covid were in their eighties or nineties? Against all this should be weighed the excess deaths, many of far younger people."[38]

The economic crisis which resulted from the lockdowns has been worse than the worst expectations, even in the West: already by March 2021, Covid measures had cost $5.2 trillion in the US, whereas World War II had cost $4.7 trillion in today's money.[39] According to Toby Green and Thomas Fazi, even in "cushioned Western countries," the "savings of the rich grew as the poor found themselves falling into rent arrears and struggling to feed their families, and a generation of poor children found their life chances scarred so deeply that many educators wonder if they will ever recover."[40] As a result of the pandemic response's "authoritarian war on the poor" and enabling of the neoliberal state, the world's billionaires had made US$4 trillion by the end of the first year of the pandemic. Toby Green calls this an "abject political surrender to the ghosts of Thatcherism" on the part of the left.[41]

Why did this tale of misery and destruction not enter Western public consciousness as the logical and predictable consequence of the lockdown? I venture that it is because the entire lockdown debate was captured by the narrative on the Covid vaccine as the upcoming savior of humanity. Indeed, it is on the vaccine issue that censorship was really rolled out.

---

com/world/2024/mar/21/young-and-ol.d-how-the-covid-pandemic-has-affected-every-uk-generation.

38 The Spectator, "Covid and the Politics of Panic."

39 Ron Surz, "Money Printing and Inflation: Covid, Cryptocurrencies, and More," *Nasdaq*, November 16, 2021, https://www.nasdaq.com/articles/money-printing-and-inflation%3A-covid-cryptocurrencies-and-more.

40 Green and Fazi, *The Covid Consensus*, 437.

41 Toby Green, "Covid-19 and the Left: A Post-Mortem," *Sublation*, May 25, 2024, https://sublationmedia.com/covid-19-and-the-left-a-postmortem/.

For instance, in 2021, the French national research agency (Centre national de la recherche scientifique, CNRS) issued a public warning to its 30,000 researchers, stating:

> The CNRS deplores the public statements made by certain scientists, often more concerned with fleeting media glory than scientific truth, on subjects far removed from their professional fields of expertise, such as vaccination against Covid. These communications do not respect any of the rules in force for scientific publications, notably peer review, which is the only way to check the rigor of the process.[42]

The CNRS was reacting here to the public statements of sociologist and biopolitical scholar Laurent Mucchielli in which he evoked the side effects of the Covid vaccine; he claimed on the basis of data from the official Vaccine Adverse Event Reporting System (VAERS) that the Covid vaccination had already by August 2021 caused the death in the US of more than five times as many people as the flu vaccine in thirty years.[43] Mucchielli was issued a call to order by CNRS despite his protests that "science is based on contradictory debate, the free discussion of data, and reasoning."[44] Science and free speech had become two contradictory notions, and Mucchielli's contentions were never discussed.

---

42 "Le CNRS exige le respect des règles de déontologie des métiers de la recherche," *CNRS.fr*, August 24, 2021, https://www.cnrs.fr/fr/presse/le-cnrs-exige-le-respect-des-regles-de-deontologie-des-metiers-de-la-recherche.

43 See Soazig Le Nevé, "Le sociologue Laurent Mucchielli rappelé à l'ordre par le CNRS," *Le Monde*, August 24, 2021, https://www.lemonde.fr/societe/article/2021/08/24/le-sociologue-laurent-mucchielli-rappele-a-l-ordre-par-le-cnrs_6092249_3224.html. The original post was taken down by Médiapart but is reproduced here: "La vaccination Covid à l'épreuve des faits—'Une mortalité inédite,'" *altermidi*, August 6, 2021, https://altermidi.org/2021/08/06/le-texte-de-laurent-mucchielli-depublier-par-mediapart/.

44 Le Nevé, "Le sociologue Laurent Mucchielli." See also his volume: Laurent Mucchielli, *La doxa du Covid: Peur, santé, corruption et démocratie*, 2 vols. (Bastia: Éoliennes, 2023).

A personal story of censorship, or how fact-checking goes wrong

On November 3, 2021, I reposted on Facebook without comment an article published by the *British Medical Journal* (*BMJ*). This article was entitled "Covid-19: Researcher Blows the Whistle on Data Integrity Issues in Pfizer's Vaccine Trial."[45] Here is the screenshot of my post:

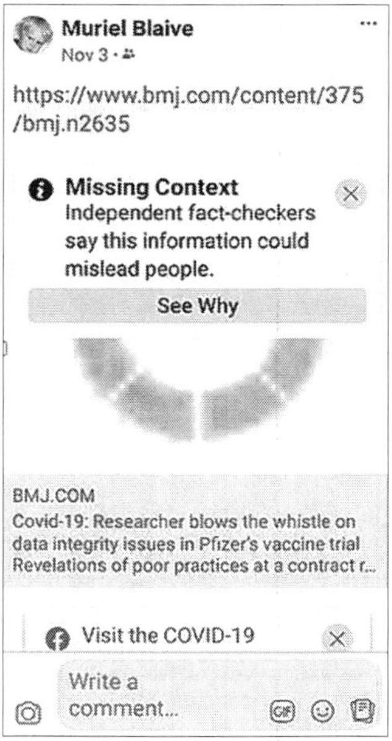

Figure 1. Screenshot of my original reposting of the *British Medical Journal* article "Covid-19: Researcher Blows the Whistle on Data Integrity Issues in Pfizer's Vaccine Trial" on Facebook, November 3, 2021

The post was instantly covered by the banner "Missing Context. Independent fact-checkers say this information could mislead people," which dwarfed it.

45 Paul D. Thacker, "Covid-19: Researcher Blows the Whistle on Data Integrity Issues in Pfizer's Vaccine Trial," *BMJ Investigation*, November 2, 2021, https://www.bmj.com/content/375/bmj.n2635.

On November 11, 2021, eight days later, I received a further notice from Facebook according to which my post had now been fully assessed by "independent fact-checkers." It was accompanied by a link toward a "related article" entitled "Fact check: The *British Medical Journal* Did NOT Reveal Disqualifying and Ignored Reports of Flaws in Pfizer COVID-19 Vaccine Trials."[46]

This article was authored by Dean Miller, the managing editor of a website called Lead Stories.[47] Lead Stories defines itself as a "fact-checking website that is always looking for the latest false, misleading, deceptive, or inaccurate stories, videos, or images going viral on the internet."[48] It is one of the companies subcontracted by Facebook to screen users' posts for misinformation, responsible at the time for up to half of Facebook's fact checks. Here is what my post now looked like—the original reference and topic were even less recognizable:

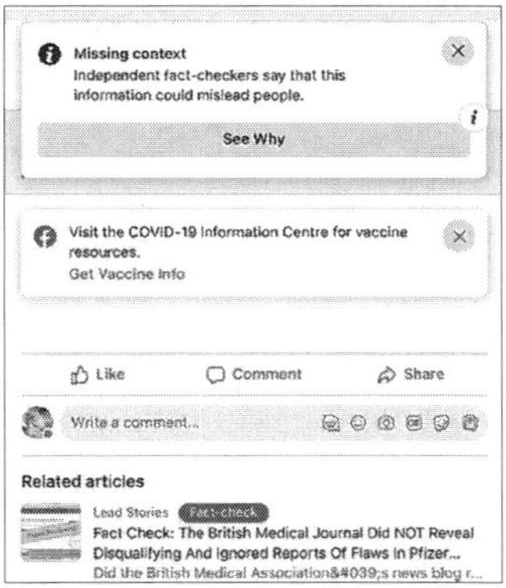

Figure 2. **Screenshot of my reposting on Facebook of the *British Medical Journal* article after it was modified by Lead Stories' "fact-check" on November 11, 2021**

46 Dean Miller, "Fact Check: The *British Medical Journal* Did NOT Reveal Disqualifying and Ignored Reports of Flaws in Pfizer COVID-19 Vaccine Trials," *Lead Stories*, November 10, 2021, https://leadstories.com/hoax-alert/2021/11/fact-check-british-medical-journal-did-not-reveal-disqualifying-and-ignored-reports-of-flaws-in-pfizer-vaccine-trial.html.

47 See his profile here: https://leadstories.com/author/dean-miller.html.

48 https://leadstories.com/.

The cancelling of this post was the result of a policy dictated by the "Trusted News Initiative," a consortium of mainstream media that focused, according to BBC Director-General Tim Davie, on "combatting the spread of harmful vaccine disinformation."[49] Launched in 2019 and reactivated on December 10, 2020, in view of the impending rollout of the Covid vaccine, it stated: "The Trusted News Initiative partners will ... work together to expand our framework and ensure legitimate concerns about future vaccinations are heard, whilst harmful disinformation myths are stopped in their tracks."[50] Founding members of the consortium were AP, AFP, BBC, CBC/Radio-Canada, European Broadcasting Union (EBU), Facebook, *Financial Times*, First Draft, Google/YouTube, *The Hindu*, Microsoft, Reuters, Reuters Institute for the Study of Journalism, Twitter, and the *Washington Post*.

A crucial question is, who is checking the fact-checkers and their definition of what is "legitimate" and "harmful"? The *BMJ* was not amused. It published on January 5, 2022, a protest letter against this Lead Stories piece which debunked the debunking.[51] This letter pointed out that the *BMJ* article was the courageous work of a whistleblower at Pfizer's as reported by journalist Paul D. Thacker and that the FB "fact-check" would have a deterring effect on future potential whistleblowers. The letter also opened up the wider issue of the way in which critics are surveilled in our societies, which is not without reminding, again, the way dissidents used to be delegitimized under communism, with arguments also pertaining at the time to public sanity and national security.

49 See BBC Media Center, "Trusted News Initiative (TNI) to Combat Spread of Harmful Vaccine Disinformation and Announces Major Research Project," *BBC*, December 10, 2020, https://www.bbc.com/mediacentre/2020/trusted-news-initiative-vaccine-disinformation.

50 BBC, "Trusted News Initiative."

51 Peter C. Gøtzsche, "Rapid Response to: Covid-19: Researcher Blows the Whistle on Data Integrity Issues in Pfizer's Vaccine Trial," *BMJ*, January 5, 2022, https://www.bmj.com/content/375/bmj.n2635/rr-86.

Journalist and lawyer Glenn Greenwald shreds to pieces this so-called "disinformation expertise":

> This is a completely fraudulent credential. It was invented out of whole cloth following the dual 2016 disasters of Brexit in the UK and Trump's victory over Hillary in the US. Seemingly out of nowhere, overnight, there descended upon the United States this creepy new group of self-anointed experts who proclaimed to the world that they were able to identify falsity and deceit where nobody else could. As a result of this unique insight they insist that they and they alone possess, they have demanded the power to dictate the limits of our political debate, and have purported to impose on the largest tech companies in the West the obligation to enforce their pronouncements.... these people are often financed by the most powerful and politically interventionist billionaires in the West. The country's largest media outlets routinely treat them as the prophets they claim to be.[52]

These fact-checkers certainly are no prophets. On the other hand, as censors, they yield enormous influence.

Unchecked fact-checking is perverse because censorship defines social capital

Dean Miller is a journalist; according to his own logic, why should he be more credentialed to assess medical data than a laboratory assistant and a science journalist, or than the *British Medical Journal* itself? Two weeks later, on January 19, 2022, the *BMJ* published a long academic response to Miller's "fact-checking" piece entitled "Facebook versus the *BMJ*:

52 Glenn Greenwald, "Lee Fang Exposes 60 Minutes's 'Disinfo Expert' as Partisan Hack," *System Update*, March 27, 2024, https://rumble.com/v4lwy9o-system-update-show-249.html.

When Fact-Checking Goes Wrong."[53] It pointed out that Dean Miller had substantiated his article with a defense that appeared to be coming straight from the horse's mouth:

> The Lead Stories article said that none of the flaws identified by *the BMJ*'s whistleblower, Brook Jackson, would "disqualify" the data collected from the main Pfizer vaccine trial. Quoting a Pfizer spokesperson, it said that the drug company had reviewed Jackson's concerns and taken "actions to correct and remediate" where necessary. A Pfizer spokesperson said that the company's investigation "did not identify any issues or concerns that would invalidate the data or jeopardize the integrity of the study."[54]

To take Pfizer at face value on such an important matter is a grave ethical and professional failure on the part of a "fact-checker." But the *BMJ* response raised yet another serious issue: Facebook refused to intervene in the matter, claiming that only fact-checkers were responsible for reviewing content and applying ratings. Conversely, Lead Stories replied that it was not responsible for Facebook's actions.[55] In this Catch-22, no one is responsible, and there was and still is no independent appeal process in place. In effect, "fact-checkers" have been granted a monopoly on information.

I posted a little communist joke to their attention: "That FB's 'independent fact-checkers' know more than the *BMJ*, in fact so much more that they can quite simply silence them, is of course the new 'science.' Facebook is the new Lysenko! (just checking if you are as good in history as you are in biology, dear FB 'independent fact-checkers.')"

---

53 Rebecca Coombes and Madlen Davies, "Facebook versus the BMJ: When Fact-Checking Goes Wrong," *BMJ*, January 19, 2022, https://www.ncbi.nlm.nih.gov/pmc/articles/PMC9893920/.

54 Coombes and Davies, "Facebook versus the BMJ."

55 Coombes and Davies, "Facebook versus the BMJ."

> **Muriel Blaive**
> 11 November 2021 ·
>
> And there we go. The other day I reposted on FB, without any comment, an article in the British Medical Journal that raised suspicions as to the integrity of the Pfizer trials. Today I received the news that my post had been checked by "independent fact-checkers" and that a "notice had been added to my post." Here is a screenshot of what my post looks like now (there is nothing left of the original post so a new reader won't even know what felony I might have "committed"), followed by a screenshot of the article I tried to repost, followed by a screenshot of the "independent article" FB now attaches to my non-existent post. In the comments I will add a screenshot of my original post.
> That FB's "independent fact-checkers" know more than the BMJ, in fact so much more that they can quite simply silence them, is of course the new "science." Facebook is the new Lysenko! (just checking if you are as good in history as you are in biology, dear FB "independent fact-checkers.")
> NB: Facebook generously offers me to delete my original post. Lol.

Figure 3. **Little communist joke addressed to the "Facebook independent fact-checkers" on November 11, 2021**

Lysenko was a Stalinist pseudo-scientist who rejected Gregor Mendel's revolutionary discoveries on genetics and who "used his political influence and power to suppress dissenting opinions and discredit, marginalize, and imprison his critics, elevating his anti-Mendelian theories to state-sanctioned doctrine."[56] Sadly, Lead Stories missed the reference and failed to censor my little joke.

On the other hand, Facebook kindly offered me to take down my post with the *BMJ* link, which was an implicit threat with consequences I did not understand fully at the time: I and all the others who refused to do so have been shadow-banned ever since. We could not be completely banned because an article in the *BMJ* is hardly "fake news," but shadow-banning was the alternative measure devised to punish those who challenged the official narrative. It means that to this day, my "Facebook friends" hardly see my posts, which then get zero or very few likes, even though I stopped posting on Covid after this incident. Since I have nowhere to appeal

56 See the Wikipedia entry on Lysenko, https://en.wikipedia.org/wiki/Trofim_Lysenko.

and the situation hasn't improved one bit in three years, I progressively migrated to Twitter, where two of my tweets reached one million impressions in my first year of active use and many others routinely hover around 20,000; this is all the difference between banning and not banning. This forced isolation made a standard user like me appear ideologically suspicious on Facebook, as opposed to appearing legitimate on Twitter. Censorship socially defines normality. Worse, it largely defines social capital.

Facebook consequently also censored my "Facebook memories" on Covid topics so even I could not see my own past posts. Those that dealt with the outbreak of the pandemic in 2020 became visible to me only in the winter of 2024. In a practice which cannot but remind of Stalinism, social media had endeavored to rewrite not only the future but also the past. Czech-French writer Milan Kundera narrates in *The Book of Laughter and Forgetting* how communist leaders who fell into disgrace were retroactively airbrushed from official pictures.[57] In one memorable scene, one such leader, Vladimír Clementis, vanished from a group picture but his hat, which he had lent to the Stalinist leader who later ordered his execution, Klement Gottwald, remained in the picture—on the leader's own head. "The struggle of man against power is the struggle of memory against forgetting," concluded Kundera.

I was silently censored on another occasion, which I hadn't even noticed until I could finally access my "Facebook memories" four years later. This time it was about masks: in May 2020, I had apparently reposted a cartoon (I still can't fully see my post) claiming that N95s and surgical masks had 95% efficiency, but cloth masks and sponge masks had 0% efficiency. Like with my other case, the banning of this post

57 See "Czechoslovakia: Falsified Photographs," *Index on Censorship* 14, no. 6 (1985): 34–39, https://journals.sagepub.com/doi/pdf/10.1080/03064228508533993.

was accompanied by an article from a fact-checking website, this time PolitiFact. I deconstructed in a short piece on my Substack channel the spurious claims of these fact-checkers as to the efficiency of cloth masks: they used "experts" to assert that cloth masks could be "up to 95% protective."[58] Since my post is still made invisible by being barred with the sign "False information. The same information was checked in another post by independent fact-checkers," I have to assume that PolitiFact still makes the claim that cloth masks can offer up to 95% protection against Covid, which is not only plain disinformation but outright dangerous to the public.

As history could have told our contemporary "fact-checkers," Stalinism is inevitably followed by destalinization. On May 13, 2024, the *Times* published a lead article, "The Times View on Press Rating Agencies: Arbiters of Truth." The self-explanatory subtitle ran: "Self-Appointed Monitors of News Accuracy Such As the Global Disinformation Index Can Undermine Objective Reporting by Penalizing Sites They Disagree with":

> The willful dissemination of inaccurate news stories by hostile foreign states and grassroots conspiracy theorists poses an obvious threat to the healthy functioning of political life. But so too does the attempt to clamp down on so-called disinformation, especially when such efforts clumsily intrude on the legitimate operations of a free press. The work of the Global Disinformation Index (GDI), a not-for-profit ratings agency founded in the UK in 2018, illustrates this chilling tendency. Though the GDI presents itself as an institution devoted to the promotion of "neutrality, independence, and transparency," in practice it has helped to stymie valuable and independent-minded journalism on the basis of little more than ideological prejudice.[59]

58 Muriel Blaive, "More Covid 'Expertise' on Facebook, More Disinformation on Masks—Still in 2024," *Muriel's Substack* (blog), May 20, 2024, https://open.substack.com/pub/murielblaive/p/more-covid-expertise-on-facebook.

59 "The Times View on Press Rating Agencies: Arbiters of Truth," *The Times*, May 13, 2024, https://www.thetimes.co.uk/article/the-times-view-on-press-ratings-agencies-arbiters-of-truth-3qg93hdnt.

The GDI was funded by the UK government until 2023, i.e., it was fully functional during Covid. In fact, the UK invested £2.6 million in it in 2020-23. Rating agencies are powerful because they act as intermediaries between online advertisers and news websites seeking advertising revenue; they "have the power to effectively starve an outlet of income if they judge it to have propagated disinformation."[60] For a small outlet, this is a question of life and death.

The US Congress has documented the attacks on free speech led by the Biden White House

On May 1, 2024, the Committee on the Judiciary and the Select Subcommittee on the Weaponization of the Federal Government of the House of Representatives published a joint interim report entitled "The Censorship-Industrial Complex: How Top Biden White House Officials Coerced Big Tech to Censor Americans, True Information, and Critics of the Biden Administration."[61] This report details the way in which Facebook, YouTube, and Amazon surrendered to demands from the White House concerning the moderation of the content published on their platforms. The respective parts of the report are called "Facebook Files," "YouTube Files," and "Amazon Files." The report did not consider Twitter but referred to the "Twitter Files" that were made public following Elon Musk's acquisition of the company, files which were already used in at least three judicial trials (see Chapter 4, section "The Covid measures are also challenged in court").

60 "The Times View."

61 Committee on the Judiciary, Select Subcommittee on the Weaponization of the Federal Government, "The Censorship-Industrial Complex: How Top Biden White House Officials Coerced Big Tech to Censor Americans, True Information, and Critics of the Biden Administration—Interim Report," Washington, DC, May 1, 2024, https://judiciary.house.gov/sites/evo-subsites/republicans-judiciary.house.gov/files/evo-media-document/Biden-WH-Censorship-Report-final.pdf.

The very title and tone of the report on the censorship-industrial complex suggest a dominating Republican influence, although the two committees are bipartisan. This in turn virtually guarantees that the report will be ignored by mainstream media. Yet, the evidence presented (subpoenaed letters, emails, messages, and other documents) is compelling. It demonstrates without a doubt that the Biden White House actively intervened to have content "moderated," i.e., censored, on these major platforms of public interest. The vaccine was always a political matter: the Democrats were suspicious of "Trump's vaccine" before winning the November 2020 election[62] but then fully endorsed the vaccine as soon as Joe Biden came into office.

The censorship of vaccine criticism is not a partisan issue. The pressure of the pharmaceutical industry to push the vaccine would have been doubtless equally strong, and the result almost certainly identical, if the president in place had been Republican rather than Democrat. But as it happens, the Covid vaccine rollout coincided with Joe Biden being in office and suited the Democrats' interventionism in Covid matters, so it is the Biden administration which became associated with what some saw as a vaccine success and others as the censorship of the vaccine failure.

While this congressional report throws an appalling light on the way any discussion of the vaccine side effects has been censored in order to push for ever more vaccinations, the present volume is too limited in size and scope to deal with the topic of the Covid vaccine itself, especially its mRNA version. I am not antivax by principle, have received all the usual shots we get in the West, and have had three shots of the Pfizer/

62 Evan Semones, "Harris Says She Wouldn't Trust Trump on Any Vaccine Released before Election," *Politico*, September 5, 2020, https://www.politico.com/news/2020/09/05/kamala-harris-trump-coronavirus-vaccine-409320.

BioNTech vaccine. My parents and my adult children are also vaccinated against Covid. However, the picture that is slowly emerging raises deep ethical concerns and would deserve a volume of its own. Since mainstream media appear paralyzed by this issue, I can only express the hope that independent journalists will continue investigating it and/or that various inquiry commissions will throw more light both on the manipulative way in which the vaccine has been presented to the public and on its potential dangers, if there are any.

What this congressional report did was to chronicle almost day by day from February to September 2021 the efforts of the Biden administration to impose its views on the three companies mentioned, until they relented and fully complied with its censorship requests. I will limit myself here to Facebook since it offers an interesting accompaniment to my experience described above.

According to the report, "Facebook began censoring in February 2021 not just anti-vaccine content but also claims that the SARS-CoV-2 virus was manmade," i.e., relating to the lab leak theory.[63] However, the Biden administration, often under the guise of Senior Pandemic Advisor Andy Slavitt or White House Press Secretary Jen Psaki, sometimes Surgeon General Vivek Murthy, continued pressuring Facebook for ever more censorship, endorsing a claim of the Center for the Countering of Digital Hate (CCDH) according to which only a dozen Facebook users, the so-called "Disinformation Dozen," were producing 65% of all anti-vaccine misinformation.[64] Internal communication at Facebook shows that the company employees were baffled by this claim, scrambled to figure out if it was true, and identified 39 suspicious accounts, while still "noting that the Biden Administration's

63 "The Censorship-Industrial Complex," 10.
64 "The Censorship-Industrial Complex," 35.

definition of 'misinformation' was 'completely unclear.'"[65] As Sheryl Sandberg, Chief Operating Officer of the company, put it, "the White House was 'scapegoating' Facebook to 'cover their own missed vaccination rates and a virus they can't get control of through public policy.'"[66] To be even more precise, communication with Surgeon-General Murthy made clear that the White House was concerned that "disinformation" on Facebook was hampering the vaccination effort.[67]

On May 26, 2021, Facebook stopped censoring the lab leak theory (although it continued demoting it until at least January 2022), but the situation escalated when President Biden told a reporter in July that "social media companies like Facebook were 'killing people' by allowing Covid misinformation to spread on their platforms."[68] On July 21, 2021, an internal memo at Facebook noted that

> the Biden White House would like Facebook to "remove content that provides any negative information on or opinions about the vaccine without concluding that the benefits of the vaccine outweigh that information or opinion" as well as "humorous or satirical content that suggests the vaccine isn't safe." The memo also indicated that it was likely that the Biden White House wanted Facebook to remove "true content and criticism of the government, both of which," the company felt the need to add, "are appropriate to allow on platform." The internal Facebook memo further explained that the Biden White House had "previously indicated that it thinks humor should be removed if it is premised on the vaccine having side effects," so Facebook "expect[ed] it would similarly want to see humor about vaccine hesitancy removed."[69]

---

65 "The Censorship-Industrial Complex," 35.
66 "The Censorship-Industrial Complex," 38.
67 "The Censorship-Industrial Complex," 37–38.
68 "The Censorship-Industrial Complex," 37.
69 "The Censorship-Industrial Complex," 43–44.

On August 18, 2021, Facebook expressed once again its frustration at the administration, noting that the oft-mentioned "Disinformation Dozen" "are responsible for about just 0.05% of all views of vaccine-related content on Facebook."[70] Yet, on August 23, 2021, it capitulated and agreed to censor what the White House demanded: "And with that, the Biden Administration's censorship campaign had completed its mission: one of the world's largest social media platforms again succumbed to pressure and violated its own principles to appease a powerful government office."[71] In a bombshell letter to Jim Jordan, Chair of the House Committee for the Judiciary, on August 26, 2024, Zuckerberg confirmed these conclusions, expressed regret, and vowed to resist such White House pressure in the future (see Chapter 4).[72]

So, this is how my reposting on Facebook of an article of the *British Medical Journal* came to be censored and my profile to be shadow-banned ever since—not because Facebook itself suspected it was disinformation, but at the request of the White House, in order to promote vaccine intake. It is all the more absurd that I (and many of those who were censored) am not antivax. Antivax people should be entitled to their opinion anyway; at the very least, should they be deprived of the right to express themselves, it should be only after a wide public debate, not at the secret whim of the executive branch in the US. To quote the report, "While the Biden White House's pressure campaign largely succeeded, its effects were devastating. By suppressing free speech and intentionally distorting public debate in the modern town

70 "The Censorship-Industrial Complex," 50.

71 "The Censorship-Industrial Complex," 50.

72 See the Twitter post of the House Judiciary GOP group, which reproduced the letter in full: House Judiciary GOP (@JudiciaryGOP), "Mark Zuckerberg just admitted three things," Twitter, August 27, 2024, 12:44 am, https://x.com/JudiciaryGOP/status/1828201780544504064.

square, ideas and policies were no longer fairly tested and debated on their merits."[73]

"Science" served to disguise hubris: the Fauci personality cult

Indeed, it is easy to claim that a "scientific consensus" reigns when anyone thinking otherwise is silenced. The primary opposition to the official Covid narrative on lockdowns, the Great Barrington Declaration,[74] which promoted focused protection and boasts almost one million signatories, was derided and defiled in the mainstream media, when it was mentioned at all. Anthony Fauci, the much-publicized director of the National Institute of Allergy and Infectious Diseases, called it "nonsense" and "dangerous."[75] As already mentioned, its three authors, Martin Kulldorff from Harvard, Sunetra Gupta from Oxford, and Jay Bhattacharya from Stanford, were called "fringe epidemiologists" by the director of the National Institutes of Health, Francis Collins.[76] Hubris followed in the footsteps of censorship: a year later and as the efficacy of lockdowns became seriously contested, Anthony Fauci claimed, "Attacks on me, quite frankly, are attacks on science."[77]

73 "The Censorship-Industrial Complex," 1.

74 See its website: https://gbdeclaration.org/.

75 Noah Higgins-Dunn, "Dr. Fauci Says Letting the Coronavirus Spread to Achieve Herd Immunity Is 'Nonsense' and 'Dangerous,'" *CNBC*, October 15, 2020, https://www.cnbc.com/2020/10/15/dr-fauci-says-letting-the-coronavirus-spread-to-achieve-herd-immunity-is-nonsense-and-dangerous.html.

76 Stephen M. Lepore, "'There Needs to Be a Quick and Devastating Take down': Emails Show How Fauci and Head of NIH Worked to Discredit Three Experts Who Penned the Great Barrington Declaration Which Called for an End to Lockdowns," *The Daily Mail*, December 19, 2021, https://www.dailymail.co.uk/news/article-10324873/Emails-reveal-Fauci-head-NIH-colluded-try-smear-experts-called-end-lockdowns.html.

77 Carlie Potterfield, "Dr. Fauci on GOP Criticism: 'Attacks on Me, Quite Frankly, Are Attacks on Science,'" *Forbes*, December 10, 2021, https://www.forbes.com/sites/carlieporterfield/2021/06/09/fauci-on-gop-criticism-attacks-on-me-quite-frankly-are-attacks-on-science/.

At the height of what reminds one of a personality cult on the communist model, the *Guardian* claimed not only that Fauci was a "superstar" and a "cult hero," but also that "the US diseases expert has been spoofed by Brad Pitt and lauded as the 'sexiest man alive.'"[78] Fauci figured on donuts from the company Donut Delite that supposedly were a "nationwide hit."[79] He posed on the cover of *InStyle* magazine wearing dark sunglasses with the caption "The Good Doctor" and the title "Dr. Fauci Says, 'With All Due Modesty, I Think I'm Pretty Effective.'"[80] His memoirs, published in 2024, advertised him as "the most famous—and most revered—doctor in the world today," making him "truly an American hero," the "embodiment of 'speaking truth to power,' with dignity and results."[81] Fauci was indeed awarded a $901,400 prize from the Israeli-based Dan David Foundation in 2021 for "speaking truth to power" and "defending science."[82]

What is science, short of being "Anthony Fauci" and his cult of the personality? How do we recognize a scientific endeavor as opposed to a political one? How do we avoid

---

78 David Smith, "'Maybe the Guy's a Masochist': How Anthony Fauci Became a Superstar," *The Guardian*, September 10, 2021, https://www.theguardian.com/film/2021/sep/10/how-anthony-fauci-became-a-superstar.

79 Lauren M. Johnson, "Doughnuts Featuring Dr. Fauci's Face Are Quickly Becoming a Nationwide Hit," *CNN*, March 26, 2020, https://edition.cnn.com/2020/03/26/us/dr-fauci-doughnuts-trnd/index.html.
See also Chris Cillizza, "Explaining the Cult of Anthony Fauci," *CNN*, April 20, 2020, https://edition.cnn.com/2020/04/20/politics/anthony-fauci-poll-favorability-trump/index.html.

80 The original article authored by Norah O'Donnell is no longer accessible. However, a review of the article can be found here: Quentin Fottrell, "Defiant Fauci Tells InStyle Magazine: 'With All Due Modesty, I Think I'm Pretty Effective,'" *MarketWatch*, July 20, 2020, https://www.marketwatch.com/story/defiant-fauci-tells-instyle-i-dont-regret-anything-i-said-and-talks-about-being-persona-non-grata-in-trumps-white-house-2020-07-17.

81 Anthony Fauci, *On Call: A Doctor's Journey in Public Service* (New York: Viking Press, 2024).

82 Nick Mordowanec, "Fauci Making Millions During COVID Pandemic Sparks Backlash," *Newsweek*, September 20, 2023, https://www.newsweek.com/fauci-making-millions-during-covid-pandemic-sparks-backlash-1828484.

sacrificing science to emotion? As I mentioned it in the introduction, for historians of communism, these are familiar questions: does historical truth even exist, and how do we recognize the work of a social scientist as opposed to an ideological argument? I mentioned Karl Popper, the philosopher of science, who pioneered a definition of the scientific method. As a young man, Popper had witnessed how the Austrian Communist Party pushed nine comrades in front of police bullets in 1919 in order to fulfill its own predictions on historical materialism and on the "worsening of the class struggle," an ideology which it claimed was "scientific." Such cynicism taught Popper that science had to be ethical in order to be protected from abuse and manipulation, and he endeavored to establish the difference between science and ideology. This is how he established the criterion of falsifiability, which places contradiction at the center of the scientific method—a criterion which was never adhered to by Covid authorities.[83]

The "science" the public was presented with was made on the fly to a large degree

When they introduced restrictions, the Western political leaders not only failed to provide any source material to subject themselves to the possibility of falsification in the Popperian sense, but they now frankly boast about the improvised form of their decision-making.[84] Mandy Cohen, future head of the CDC, at the time North Carolina Health Director, laughed in 2024 about deciding on the phone in 2020, seem-

83 See Friedel Weinert, *Karl Popper: Professional Philosopher and Public Intellectual* (Cham: Springer, 2022), 13–14.

84 See the Twitter thread provided by user Ian Solliec (@IanSolliec), "Each time we lift a veil of government, it's obvious that none of them were ever 'following the science,'" Twitter, March 22, 2024, 8:10 am, https://twitter.com/IanSolliec/status/1771071883770753251.

ingly on a whim, to "close down sports," as seen on a video posted on Twitter.[85] Matt Hancock, the UK Health Secretary, was enraged in 2020 by the "f...ing Sweden argument" and demanded "a few bullet points to quash it."[86] Francis Collins, the head of the National Institutes of Health in the U.S., ordered as already mentioned a "devastating takedown" of the Great Barrington Declaration.[87] Nicola Sturgeon, as First Minister of Scotland, decided to mask children in schools on a political rather than medical basis, yet Prime Minister Johnson decided it was "not worth an argument" with her, as later testified by his Chief Scientific Advisor Patrick Vallance during the UK Covid Inquiry.[88] Gabriel Attal, later French Prime Minister and at the time government spokesperson, admitted that the vaccine passports were not based on science but on "hope."[89]

In Germany, the Robert Koch Institute (RKI) deliberately ignored the data which was contradicting its theory, while its decision-making was political and erratic.[90] As late as October

---

85 See Laura Powell (@LauraPowellEsq), "As NC health director, @DrMandyCohen felt comfortable wielding dictatorial power," Twitter, June 2, 2023, 1:12 am, https://twitter.com/LauraPowellEsq/status/1664409518468653056.

86 See Fraser Nelson, "Britain Was Failed by a Pro-Lockdown Clique Incapable of Admitting Its Errors," *The Telegraph*, March 2, 2023, https://www.telegraph.co.uk/news/2023/03/02/britain-failed-pro-lockdown-clique-incapable-admitting-errors/.

87 See the email here: Phil Magness (@PhilWMagness), "New email dump showing Anthony Fauci and Francis Collins coordinating a propaganda campaign," Twitter, December 17, 2021, 10:33 pm, https://twitter.com/PhilWMagness/status/1471956647266377736.

88 Simon Johnson, "Sturgeon Making Children Wear Masks Was Political, Sir Patrick Vallence Wrote in Covid Diary," *The Telegraph*, March 12, 2024, https://www.telegraph.co.uk/news/2024/03/12/sturgeon-masks-schools-political-scotland-vallance-covid/.

89 See his appearance on TV channel CNews (@CNEWS) "Gabriel Attal: 'Je ne crois pas qu'on se soit trompé sur l'efficacité du vaccin,'" Twitter, February 16, 2022, 8:22 pm, https://twitter.com/CNEWS/status/1494029451662970886.

90 See Stefan Korinth and Paul Schreyer, "Mehr als tausend Passagen geschwärzt: Multipolar veröffentlicht freigeklagte RKI-Protokolle im Original," *Multipolar*,

30, 2020, it claimed that "FFP2 masks are an occupational safety measure. If people are not trained/qualified personnel, FFP2 masks have no added value if they are not fitted and used correctly,"[91] yet the mask was made compulsory only a few weeks later. On January 8, 2021, it claimed that the AstraZeneca vaccine "needed to be discussed" and there "may need to be restrictions," yet two months later the vaccine was recommended for all age groups.[92] On March 5, 2021, the RKI confirmed that vaccination status should never be a pretext for restrictions; yet in mid-September 2021, the "3G rule" (vaccinated, recovered, tested) was added to official restrictions.[93] The serious daily *Die Welt* eventually stated that the Robert Koch protocols had proven that "politics ignored science" and that the would-be scientific consensus around Covid was predicated on silencing dissenting scientists.[94]

Concerning masks, journalist Paul D. Thacker remarked that the companies which produce them still carefully advertise on the box that masks "do not stop communicable diseases"—and should therefore be rather understood as a tribal, political statement than as a medical device.[95] In a video for the

---

March 20, 2024, https://multipolar-magazin.de/artikel/rki-protokolle-2.

91 Britta Spikermann, "Die brisanten Corona-Protokolle des RKI," *ZDF*, March 23, 2024, https://www.zdf.de/nachrichten/politik/deutschland/rki-protokolle-corona-klagen-100.html.

92 Spikermann, "Die brisanten Corona-Protokolle."

93 Spikermann, "Die brisanten Corona-Protokolle."

94 Tim Röhn and Anna Kröning, "Die RKI-Protokolle und wie die Politik die Wissenschaft ignorierte," *Die Welt*, March 26, 2024, https://www.welt.de/politik/deutschland/plus250755780/Corona-Die-RKI-Protokolle-und-wie-die-Politik-die-Wissenschaft-ignorierte.html. See also David Averre, "Lockdowns Could Cause More Harm Than Covid-19 and There Was No Evidence That Wearing Masks Was Useful, German Health Body Admitted during Coronavirus Pandemic, Released Documents Show," *The Daily Mail*, March 26, 2024, https://www.dailymail.co.uk/news/article-13239595/Lockdowns-cause-harm-Covid-19-no-evidence-wearing-masks-useful-German-health-body-admitted-coronavirus-pandemic-released-documents-show.html.

95 See Jay Bhattacharya, "Episode 35: Paul Thacker on the Illusion of Consensus

Independent, an expert tried out various combinations of masks (cloth, surgical, and FFP2) separately and combined with each other against the sun in a cold environment. The moisture on which the virus circulates was clearly visible in every combination. Against his own evidence, the expert concluded that this was proof that wearing two FFP2 masks on top of each other "worked."[96] Even if that had been true (it clearly wasn't), it was never realistic to expect that the population at large would wear two FFP2 masks on top of one another at all times and would change them regularly. Meanwhile, he convincingly demonstrated that wearing any one mask at a time was useless.

The definitive answer to the potential usefulness or uselessness of masks should have been provided by the Cochrane study on the topic. Cochrane is generally considered the highest quality standard in medical research because it examines all studies put together. A Cochrane study on NPIs to stop Covid, including masks, did appear in 2023 and concluded that "wearing a mask may make little or no difference in how many people caught a flu-like illness/Covid-like illness."[97] Crucially, the study noted that too few randomized controlled trials had been carried out so far and many more were needed. But the public outcry was such—the study indeed delegitimized the dominant public health message—that Karla Soares-Weiser, the editor-in-chief of the Cochrane Library, felt compelled to backtrack. She stated that "masks don't work" would be

---

of Masking," *The Illusion of Consensus* (podcast), March 10, 2024, https://www.illusionconsensus.com/p/episode-35-paul-thacker-on-the-illusion.

96 "Expert Demonstrates Efficacy of Double Masks in Cold Weather," *The Independent TV*, YouTube video, 1:41, February 21, 2021, https://www.youtube.com/watch?v=_fPfGU1MizY.

97 Tom Jefferson et. al., "Physical Interventions to Interrupt or Reduce the Spread of Respiratory Viruses," *Cochrane Review*, January 30, 2023, https://www.cochranelibrary.com/cdsr/doi/10.1002/14651858.CD006207.pub6/full.

an "inaccurate and misleading interpretation" of the study.[98] This retraction, dubbed a fiasco by many and angering the lead author of the study, who was not consulted, caused a fresh new scandal in the scientific community and further contributed to politicizing the mask issue.[99]

As to the "six feet apart" (or two meters in Europe) social distancing recommendation, it was not based on any scientific evidence but "just sort of appeared," according to Fauci, as he testified to the House of Representatives Select Subcommittee on the Coronavirus Pandemic on January 10, 2024. He acknowledged by the same token that the lab leak hypothesis was no conspiracy theory but a distinct possibility.[100] New studies in 2024 also showed that the top medical journals had been heavily biased towards the "Zero Covid" strategy by publishing 272 papers from authors supporting it in the UK alone, against 21 from authors with a more critical view and only six from authors of the Great Barrington Declaration.[101]

Anthony Fauci also dubiously moved the goalpost for achieving "herd immunity," which was considered to be around 60% of the population if vaccinated, to 80%-85% on a whim ("I thought, 'I can nudge this up a bit,' so I went to 80, 85.").[102]

---

98 "Statement on 'Physical Interventions to Interrupt or Reduce the Spread of Respiratory Viruses' Review," *Cochrane Review*, March 10, 2023, https://www.cochrane.org/news/statement-physical-interventions-interrupt-or-reduce-spread-respiratory-viruses-review.

99 See the blog post of Vinay Prasad, "The Cochrane Mask Fiasco," *Sensible Medicine* (blog), March 15, 2023, https://www.sensible-med.com/p/the-cochrane-mask-fiasco.

100 See the Twitter post of this Select Subcommittee (@COVIDSelect), "Dr. Fauci claimed that the '6 feet apart' social distancing recommendation promoted by federal health officials was likely not based on any data," Twitter, January 10, 2024, 12;41 pm, https://twitter.com/COVIDSelect/status/1745048323852005634.

101 Kevin Bardosh, "Top Medical Journals Were Biased towards Zero Covid, Studies Find," *UnHerd*, June 20, 2024, https://unherd.com/newsroom/top-medical-journals-were-biased-towards-zero-covid-studies-find/.

102 Vinay Prasad, "Why Did Fauci Move the Herd Immunity Goal Posts? Scientists

These are only select examples, and the list is much longer. Such a list naturally raises the question of the validity of science and expertise, which I will further examine in Chapter 3.

Summary of Chapter 2

Chapter 2 delved into the collateral damage, censorship, and hubris experienced during the Covid lockdowns, focusing on the neglect of suffering in the developing world caused by Western responses. It highlighted how the lockdowns disproportionately affected the poor and vulnerable globally, leading to increased hunger, economic devastation, and a myriad of social and health crises. Despite warnings and evidence of the adverse effects of lockdowns, policymakers persisted, causing long-term harm to education, mental health, and economic stability. The chapter also critiqued the response of the Western liberal left, which, despite its purported commitment to social justice, displayed its indifference to the inequalities exacerbated by lockdown measures not only in the developing world but also at home. Furthermore, it discussed the censorship of dissenting voices, particularly regarding vaccine skepticism, and the way in which the focus on vaccines overshadowed discussions on the broader impact of lockdown policies. It raised broader concerns about the suppression of dissenting voices and the influence of powerful actors like the Biden administration in shaping public discourse.

Play a Dangerous Game When They Tailor Factual Statements to Promote Policy Goals," *MedPageToday*, December 29, 2020, https://www.medpagetoday.com/opinion/vinay-prasad/90445.

Chapter 3

The Instrumentalization of Science and Expertise during Covid

> Whenever a theory appears to you as the only possible one, take this as a sign that you have neither understood the theory nor the problem which it was intended to solve.
>
> Karl Popper, *Objective Knowledge: An Evolutionary Approach*

> The disappearance of a sense of responsibility is the most far-reaching consequence of submission to authority.
>
> Stanley Milgram, *Obedience to Authority*

During an (in)famous research study on human obedience at Yale University in 1961-65, sociologist Stanley Milgram submitted subjects to his authority as a "scientist" in his laboratory and led them with disconcerting ease to torture others under the reassuring pretext that they were following orders and working for the good of science.[1] The study was unethical and was criticized as such, but it showed we tend to believe white coats no matter what they say.

This is why it is crucial to know what science and experts are. Just as in the case of Lead Stories, PolitiFact, and the Trusted News Initiative, mainstream media and their fight against disinformation have not always been helpful but have rather confused matters: "An entire industry of journalists, academics, and experts has arisen to hunt down, track, and

1 See Stanley Milgram, "Behavioral Study of Obedience," *Journal of Abnormal and Social Psychology* 67, no. 4 (1963): 371–78.

police misinformation. In some ways, this industry is just as creepy and alarming as the conspiracy culture it gorges on, mirroring its familiar pathologies of distortion and hyperbole."[2]

Not only was the notion of expertise abused during Covid, but few if any of the mainstream media seem to have pondered the possibility that the consulted experts themselves were under peer pressure and financial constraint to support the vaccine narrative. The American Hospital Association revealed, for instance, that it received three grants from the CDC to "support Covid-19 vaccine confidence" from 2021 to 2023, totaling 4.5 million dollars, specifically via running "public service announcements, newspaper advertisements, and radio spots" in English and Spanish; releasing educational videos and podcasts; convening events; and publishing more than 100 case studies on "vaccine successes."[3]

The US government also used churches to convey its pro-Covid vaccine message, which caused some fury in the Christian communities when this was discovered.[4] It similarly allocated $219.5 million in 2020 and 2021 to tribal communities in the Indian Country in order to "support tribes and tribal organizations in carrying out surveillance, epidemiology, laboratory capacity, infection control, mitigation, communication, and other COVID-19 preparedness and response activities."[5]

2 Simon Cottee, "The hypocrisy of the BBC's Misinformation War," *UnHerd*, March 7, 2024, https://unherd.com/2024/03/the-hypocrisy-of-the-bbcs-misinformation-war/.

3 See AHA, "AHA Receives $1.5 Million CDC Grant to Build Vaccine Confidence, Partner with Children's Hospital Association," October 20, 2022, https://www.aha.org/press-releases/2022-10-20-aha-receives-15-million-cdc-grant-build-vaccine-confidence-partner-childrens-hospital-association.

4 Megan Basham, "How the Federal Government Used Evangelical Leaders to Spread Covid Propaganda to Churches," *The Daily Wire*, February 1, 2022, https://www.dailywire.com/news/how-the-federal-government-used-evangelical-leaders-to-spread-covid-propaganda-to-churches.

5 Centers for Disease Control and Prevention (CDC), "CDC COVID-19 Funding for Tribes," August 15, 2021, https://www.cdc.gov/tribal-health/cooperative-agreements/documents/ot20-2004/COVID_Funding_Tribes_062021.pdf.

The media did not seem to really factor in either that a number of large social media influencers (more than 50 according to the *New York Times*), as well as an "eclectic army" of small media influencers who were paid $1,000 a month (it is not specified for how long), were hired to "reach vaccine skeptics and dispel myths."[6] This $250 million campaign was funded by the White House in order to achieve the 75% to 80% vaccination rate which would allow society to reach herd immunity,[7] a number made up on the fly by Anthony Fauci, as seen in Chapter 2.

The *New York Times* reported on this recruiting campaign, led by the same Anthony Fauci, taking the example of Christina Najjar, a TikTok "star" known as Tinx:

> Discussing what she called a "happy vaxx girl summer," Ms. Najjar peppered Dr. Fauci with questions: Was it safe to go out for a drink? Should we be concerned about getting pregnant after getting the vaccine? Do I look 26? "You have an ageless look to you," he replied.
>
> "I'll tell my Botox doctor that," she said.
>
> Ms. Najjar called the session "a great time," adding, "I think I flirted with Dr. Fauci, but in a respectful way." A White House official said Dr. Fauci was not available for comment.[8]

---

6 The Guardian Staff, "US Recruits Social Media Influencers to Reach Vaccine Sceptics and Dispel Myths," *The Guardian*, August 11, 2021, https://www.theguardian.com/us-news/2021/aug/11/us-recruits-social-media-influencers-reach-vaccine-skeptics.

7 See Graham Kates, "Inside the $250 Million Effort to Convince Americans the Coronavirus Vaccines Are Safe," *CBS News*, December 23, 2020, https://www.cbsnews.com/news/covid-vaccine-safety-250-million-dollar-marketing-campaign/.

8 Taylor Lorenz, "To Fight Vaccine Lies, Authorities Recruit an 'Influencer Army,'" *The New York Times*, August 1, 2021, https://www.nytimes.com/2021/08/01/technology/vaccine-lies-influencer-army.html.

A quality outlet such as the *New York Times* apparently considered this exchange newsworthy, all the while refraining from investigating the financial ties between public health institutions and the pharmaceutical industry.

The capture of public health by the pharmaceutical industry

The Covid pandemic has revealed the extent to which the pharmaceutical industry has captured public health in the US, the UK, and the EU:[9] 89% of the European Medicines Agency funding comes from the industry, up from a mere 20% in 1995; 86% of the UK Medicines and Healthcare Regulatory Agency; and 65% of the US Food and Drug Administration (a 30-fold increase since 1992), including 75% of the Food and Drug Administration's Drug Division.[10] As a result and unsurprisingly, "Analysis in the US, where before the 1992 Act the FDA was a fully taxpayer-funded entity, has shown that 'reliance on industry fees is contributing to a decline in evidentiary standards, ultimately harming patients.'"[11]

This matters because when this industry decides to sell a particular medicine or vaccine, it holds considerable sway not only over regulatory agencies but over mainstream media: 75% of TV advertisement spending in the US in 2020, for instance, came from the pharmaceutical industry;[12] and

9 See Sheena Meredith, "'Institutional Corruption' Permeates Drug Regulators Globally," *Medscape UK*, June 30, 2022, https://www.medscape.co.uk/viewarticle/institutional-corruption-permeates-drug-regulators-globally-2022a1001obx. See also the excellent episode from Jay Bhattacharya, "How Pharmaceutical Companies Control the Narrative, with Sharyl Attkisson," *The Illusion of Consensus* (podcast), September 11, 2024, https://www.illusionconsensus.com/p/how-pharmaceutical-companies-control.

10 Christina Jewett, "F.D.A.'s Drug Industry Fees Fuel Concerns over Influence," *The New York Times*, September 15, 2022, https://www.nytimes.com/2022/09/15/health/fda-drug-industry-fees.html.

11 Meredith, "Institutional Corruption."

12 Michelle Majidi, "Pharmaceutical Industry TV Advertising Spending in the United States from 2016 to 2020," *Statista.com*, December 20, 2023, https://

over MPs as well, as the *Guardian* showed in the case of the UK.[13] As for the Covid vaccine, another US public agency, the National Institutes of Health, claims to have co-invented it[14] and thus to hold a share in the patent;[15] hence, it has stood from the start to make a considerable amount of money with the vaccine it is recommending to the public as a supposedly independent authority. It received a first payment of $400 million from Moderna in 2023[16] and is still engaged in another lawsuit with Moderna over this patent issue.[17] As this book was going into print, the NIH additionally closed a deal with BioNTech, the firm partnered with Pfizer, to receive $791.5 million in Covid vaccine royalty payments.[18]

In France, the consulting firm McKinsey was contracted out by the government to help define its vaccination strategy.[19] The French Senate Commission of Inquiry concluded that a "massive intervention by McKinsey in the vaccination campaign" had taken place for almost a year:

McKinsey consultants worked on central subjects such as

www.statista.com/statistics/953104/pharma-industry-tv-ad-spend-us/.

13 Denis Campbell, "Drug Firms Giving MPs 'Hidden' Funding, Research Shows," *The Guardian*, June 25, 2021, https://www.theguardian.com/business/2021/jun/25/drug-firms-giving-mps-hidden-funding-research-shows.

14 "NIH Contributions to WHO COVID-19 Technology Access Pool and Q&As," *NIH*, May 12, 2022, https://www.techtransfer.nih.gov/policy/ctap.

15 Christopher Rowland, "Moderna Took NIH Money and Help for Its Covid Vaccine. Now It Wants to Leave Government Scientists off a Lucrative Patent," *The Washington Post*, November 9, 2021, https://www.washingtonpost.com/business/2021/11/09/moderna-nih-patent-vaccine/.

16 Benjamin Mueller, "After Long Delay, Moderna Pays N.I.H. for Covid Vaccine Technique," *The New York Times*, February 23, 2023, https://www.nytimes.com/2023/02/23/science/moderna-covid-vaccine-patent-nih.html.

17 Sheryl Gay Stolberg and Rebecca Robbins, "Moderna and U.S. at Odds over Vaccine Patent Rights," *The New York Times*, November 11, 2021, https://www.nytimes.com/2021/11/09/us/moderna-vaccine-patent.html.

18 Reuters, "BioNTech enters settlement with US agency, UPenn over COVID vaccine royalties," December 27, 2024, https://www.reuters.com/business/healthcare-pharmaceuticals/biontech-enters-settlement-with-us-agency-upenn-over-covid-vaccine-royalties-2024-12-27/.

19 Liz Alderman, "France Hired McKinsey to Help in the Pandemic. Then Came the Questions," *The New York Times*, February 22, 2021, https://www.nytimes.com/2021/02/22/business/france-mckinsey-consultants-covid-vaccine.html.

> monitoring and projection of vaccine deliveries and injections, analysis of appointment bookings, support for the organization of the vaccination task force, etc. They also participated in the development of documents up to the top of the state, including for the Defense and National Security Council (CDSN, see below.)
>
> Generally speaking, this case study demonstrates that key issues of the health crisis have been subcontracted to consulting firms, even creating a form of dependence of the state on said firms.[20]

This influence of McKinsey on the French administration is compounded by the links between several individual actors:

- between President Macron and McKinsey, the latter having organized his first presidential campaign[21] and still "helping," reportedly "for free;"[22]
- between the president of the Constitutional Court, Laurent Fabius, and McKinsey, since Laurent Fabius's son, Victor Fabius, is Associate Director of McKinsey France, which did make it less likely that the Constitutional Court would disavow the freedom-depriving "Health Pass"

20 Arnaud Bazin, Eliane Assassi, "Un phénomène tentaculaire: l'influence croissante des cabinets de conseils sur les politiques publiques—Rapport," Sénat—Rapport de commission d'enquête n°578 (2021-2022), *Sénat.fr*, March 16, 2022, https://www.senat.fr/rap/r21-578-1/r21-578-124.html.

21 Les Décodeurs and Service société, "French Prosecutors Investigate McKinsey's Role in Macron's Presidential Campaign," *Le Monde*, November 25, 2022, https://www.lemonde.fr/en/politics/article/2022/11/25/french-prosecutors-investigate-mckinsey-s-role-into-macron-s-presidential-campaigns_6005636_5.html.

22 "Covid-19: on vous résume la polémique autour de McKinsey, le cabinet qui conseille le gouvernement sur la stratégie vaccinale," *France Info*, February 10, 2021, https://www.francetvinfo.fr/sante/maladie/coronavirus/vaccin/covid-19-on-vous-resume-la-polemique-autour-de-mckinsey-le-cabinet-qui-conseille-le-gouvernement-sur-la-strategie-vaccinale_4291131.html.

recommended by McKinsey during Covid;[23]

- between McKinsey and prominent pharmaceutical firms, including Pfizer: for an example from another country, Pfizer hired prominent McKinsey executives in the midst of the pandemic,[24] and McKinsey not only advised the government in Quebec on vaccination strategy but simultaneously worked for Pfizer as well, a conflict of interest which it attempted to hide from the Quebec government;[25]
- between President Macron and Pfizer, since at the time when he worked in the Rothschild Bank Macron advised Nestlé on the purchase of Pfizer's nutrition division.[26]

What deserves to be asked in this context is if the narrative of fear the public was submitted to concerning Covid on the part of health regulatory agencies was entirely neutral and devoid of interest. One answer could be: Covid was dangerous, but the public health narrative was disproportionately dramatized with the intent to sell an upcoming vaccine put together at lightning speed, moreover a vaccine from which

23 Vincent Coquaz and Danae Corte, "Conseil constitutionnel et pass sanitaire: Laurent Fabius est-il en situation de conflit d'intérêts à cause de son fils chez McKinsey?" *Libération*, August 8, 2021, https://www.liberation.fr/checknews/conseil-constitutionnel-et-pass-sanitaire-laurent-fabius-est-il-en-situation-de-conflit-dinterets-a-cause-de-son-fils-chez-mckinsey-20210808_ORZB5IZ3CNBNVPICGOXSHDIA4A/.

24 McKinsey executives such as Amir Malik joined Pfizer: "Pfizer Announces New Chief Business Innovation Officer," Pfizer.com, August 26, 2021, https://www.pfizer.com/news/press-release/press-release-detail/pfizer-announces-new-chief-business-innovation-officer.

25 Jacob Serebrin, "CAQ Leader Defends Paying Millions to US Consulting Firms during Pandemic," *CBC*, September 30, 2022, https://www.cbc.ca/news/canada/montreal/caq-legault-mckinsey-pandemic-consulting-1.6602374.

26 Matthieu van Berchem, "Macron, le 'banquier de Nestlé' à l'Elysée?," *Swissinfo.ch*, May 4, 2017, https:/www.swissinfo.ch/fre/economie/election-pr%c3%a9sidentielle-fran%c3%a7aise_macron-le-banquier-de-nestl%c3%a9-%c3%a0-l-elys%c3%a9e/43153142.

health authorities were to profit. Jay Bhattacharya recalls the fact that anyone proposing to try any other medicine[27] or to trust natural immunity[28] was derided as mistaken; anyone attempting to question the stringency of the response was branded a "granny killer";[29] anyone daring to question the wisdom of mandating a hastily tested vaccine was thought to have "lost the plot."[30] The virus was deadly and only the vaccine would save the public.[31]

It is not the purpose of this volume to entirely deconstruct the influence of the pharmaceutical industry on various governments, a task which serious mainstream media should have embarked upon long ago.[32] I only wish to point out in this section that it is an issue which deserves thorough investigation, and much of this information is readily available. Which begs yet again the question why mainstream media have so far declined to get down to business. Certainly, many of these media outlets themselves enjoy funding from the pharmaceutical industry, which places them in a position of conflict of interest. But I would also venture the thesis that

---

27 Scott Sayare, "He Was a Science Star. Then He Promoted a Questionable Cure for Covid-19," *The New York Times*, May 12, 2020, https://www.nytimes.com/2020/05/12/magazine/didier-raoult-hydroxychloroquine.html.

28 Ian Sample, "Previous Covid Infection May Not Offer Long-Term Protection, Study Finds," *The Guardian*, June 17, 2021, https://www.theguardian.com/world/2021/jun/17/previous-covid-infection-may-not-offer-long-term-protection-study-finds.

29 David Mercer, "Coronavirus: Young People Warned 'Don't Kill Granny' As Lockdown Measures Reimposed in Preston," *Sky News*, August 9, 2020, https://news.sky.com/story/coronavirus-young-people-warned-dont-kill-granny-as-lockdown-imposed-in-preston-12045017.

30 Aaron Blake, "The GOP's Top Vaccine Skeptics Have Lost the Plot," *The Washington Post*, August 11, 2021, https://www.washingtonpost.com/politics/2021/08/11/gops-top-vaccine-skeptics-have-completely-lost-plot/.

31 "Benefits of Getting Vaccinated," *CDC*, September 22, 2023, https://www.cdc.gov/coronavirus/2019-ncov/vaccines/vaccine-benefits.html.

32 Others have started to do so. See, for instance, Laurent Mucchielli, *La Doxa du Covid*, vol. 1, *Peur, santé, corruption et démocratie* (Bastia: Éoliennes, 2022), in particular the chapter "Un grand projet de vaccination pour toute l'humanité."

the strong adherence to the Covid narrative in mainstream liberal media is understood as an "anti-Trump" narrative with the same fervor as the "anti-fascist" movement once bound progressive forces in the interwar and postwar periods. This prevents them from criticizing the industry because it might rapidly amount to criticizing the vaccine, which has become an absolute taboo among Western liberals.

Mainstream media are quite supportive of the increasing crackdown on social media in the West also because it gives them an edge over a competitor that has done nothing but challenge their social relevance, intellectual acumen, and sources of funding in the past years. Needless to say, this support for authoritarianism is very shortsighted—once social media are tamed, mainstream media will be next in line if they ever venture to criticize governments. But the pandemic has shown that few individuals in positions of responsibility are still able to think ahead, if only by a few months.

It might be useful to recall, however, that the same left also has a history of picking the wrong battles. In Germany of the 1920s and 1930s, the communist party (the progressive force of the time) was so intent on destroying their social-democratic rivals that they rather sacrificed them than rally with them against the Nazis—thereby helping the Nazis to get into power and liquidate them both together. To designate any critic of the Covid narrative today as the equivalent of the former "fascist enemy" is to similarly favor the extreme right while curbing the only allies of the liberal left.

Moreover, the notion of "expertise" was abused to further the official narrative on Covid. Two figures played a key role in March 2020 in this respect: Neil Ferguson and Tomas Pueyo, but first I will examine the Czech case as a lesser known example of Covid "expertise."

Roman Prymula: Conflicts of interest, racial genetics, and rule flouting

In the Czech Republic, army colonel and head of the Covid task force, epidemiologist Roman Prymula, previously served as hospital director in the university town of Hradec Králové from 2009 to 2016. During his tenure, he surprised Czech medical authorities by promoting the establishment of a traditional Chinese medicine clinic, funded by a Chinese company through an endowment trust. He attached it to the hospital under his command, arguing that Chinese medicine was a useful complement to Western medicine. The Ethics Committee of the Czech Chamber of Medicine disagreed and closed the center in 2019.[33] Meanwhile, however, Prymula himself had been relieved from his position by the Czech Health Minister due to an accusation of conflict of interest involving the firm Biovomed, owned by his daughter but conducting medical research sponsored by public authorities.[34]

From 2017 to 2020, Prymula served as Deputy Minister of Health despite facing obstacles from the Czech National Security Office, which declined to grant him a security clearance, likely due to his connections with China. Nevertheless, he was appointed chairman of the Covid Crisis Staff in mid-March 2020, emerging as a key figure of the hardline stance against Covid. Acting as the Czech equivalent of Francis Collins, he argued for a stringent mask policy and harsh lockdown.

---

33 "Centrum čínské medicíny v Hradci končí. Vedoucí bude dále provádět akupunkturu," *Aktualne.cz*, February 11, 2019, https://zpravy.aktualne.cz/domaci/centrum-cinske-mediciny-v-hradci-konci-vedouci-bude-dale-pro/r~fe2742802dd611e99182ac1f6b220ee8/.

34 Čeněk Třeček and Jan Nevyhoštěný "Šéf hradecké nemocnice Prymula končí. Kvůli obchodům s firmou své dcery," *iDnes*, June 30, 2016, https://www.idnes.cz/zpravy/domaci/minist-odvolal-reditel-fn-hradec-kralove-roman-prymula.A160630_145424_domaci_hro.

In April 2020, at a time when the Czech Republic was relatively unaffected by the pandemic and Germany was doing better than many other Western European states, Prymula raised eyebrows by suggesting that "race" might play a role in this double apparent success. He marveled at the fact that "Germanic peoples," a term seldom heard since the departure of Nazi occupation troops in 1945, "seem(ed) to be more resilient to the virus than Southern nations," a happy coincidence since "Czechs are one-third Germanic."[35] The argument proved rather moot when the Czech Republic eventually ended in the worst quarter of Europe as far as Covid mortality went.[36]

In September 2020, Prymula's expertise earned him the position of Czech Minister of Health. However, his tenure was short-lived. On October 22, 2020, he was photographed leaving a restaurant at a time when restaurants were closed for lockdown on his own orders, and notably without wearing a mask while in the company of several individuals, despite having made masks mandatory in public.[37] He was removed from his position as Health Minister but was appointed as Covid expert to the Prime Minister.[38]

---

35 JAF, "Prymula: Zdá se, že Germáni jsou odolnější než jižní národy. A Češi jsou ze třetiny Germáni," *Echo24*, April 11, 2024, https://echo24.cz/a/SeAKd/prymula-zda-se-ze-germani-jsou-odolnejsi-nez-jizni-narody-a-cesi-jsou-ze-tretiny-germani.

36 For a comparative panel of Covid mortality per capita, see https://ourworldindata.org/explorers/coronavirus-data-explorer?zoomToSelection=true&time=2020-02-03..latest&region=Europe&facet=none&country=ISR~PSE~FRA~ITA~SVN~BEL~CZE~SVK~HUN~USA~GBR~EuropeanUnion~~DEU~AUT~European+Union~OWID_WRL~POL~BIH~BRA~NOR~PRT~NLD~NZL~JPN~UKR~HKG~CHN~SWE~KEN&pickerSort=asc&pickerMetric=location&hideControls=true&Metric=Confirmed+deaths&Interval=Cumulative&Relative+to+Population=true&Color+by+test+positivity=false.

37 Kub, "Prymula bude dál pandemii řešit jako vládní expert," *Novinky.cz*, October 25, 2020, https://www.novinky.cz/clanek/domaci-prymula-se-bude-do-reseni-pandemie-zapojovat-na-expertni-urovni-40340355.

38 Kub, "Prymula bude dál pandemii řešit."

The saga continued the following day when it was disclosed that Prymula's daughter was now at the helm of another company that had received a significant state subsidy to produce disinfectant. Despite the subsidy, the company exhibited "minimal activity" and was "mostly operating at a loss."[39]

Prymula's tumultuous politico-medical journey reached its climax in February 2021 when he was spotted attending an international football match in Prague, despite strict lockdown measures he himself had advocated. His defense that he hadn't taken any vacation that year fell flat, especially given his earlier proclamation that day that he intended to recommend even stricter lockdown measures to the Prime Minister due to the worsening epidemic situation. He was dismissed from his role as a public health expert.[40]

Neil Ferguson: "Professor Lockdown," a doomsday predictor

Neil Ferguson, a British epidemiologist and professor at Imperial College London, is an expert in mathematical modeling of infectious disease patterns. His report, "Impact of Non-Pharmaceutical Interventions (NPIs) to Reduce COVID-19 Mortality and Healthcare Demand,"[41] released on March 16,

---

39 ČTK, "Firma Prymulovy dcery získala dotaci k výrobě dezinfekce," *Novinky.cz*, October 24, 2020, https://www.novinky.cz/clanek/domaci-firma-prymulovy-dcery-ziskala-dotaci-k-vyrobe-dezinfekce-40340313.

40 "Prymula k účasti na fotbale: To mám být jen doma?" *Novinky.cz*, February 18, 2021, https://www.novinky.cz/clanek/domaci-prymula-k-ucasti-na-fotbale-to-mam-byt-jen-doma-40351494.

41 Neil Ferguson et. al., "Impact of Non-Pharmaceutical Interventions (NPIs) to Reduce COVID-19 Mortality and Healthcare Demand," Imperial College Covid-19 Response Team, March 16, 2020, https://www.imperial.ac.uk/media/imperial-college/medicine/sph/ide/gida-fellowships/Imperial-College-COVID19-NPI-modelling-16-03-2020.pdf.

2020, garnered global attention.[42] The findings of Ferguson's report prompted Prime Minister Boris Johnson to pivot away from the strategy of pursuing "herd immunity" and implement instead a strict lockdown. Moreover, it provided governments around the world with the scientific rationale to impose lockdowns and mask mandates as crucial measures in combating the pandemic, although the model itself was little discussed or critiqued.[43]

The report predicted a staggering number of deaths in the absence of interventions: "In total, in an unmitigated epidemic, we would predict approximately 510,000 deaths in GB and 2.2 million in the US, not accounting for the potential negative effects of health systems being overwhelmed on mortality."[44] When adapted to Sweden by a team from Uppsala University, the model predicted 96,000 deaths by the end of June 2020 without lockdowns and stringent NPIs, a scenario labeled as a "catastrophe."[45] In fact, by that date, Sweden counted 5,416 Covid deaths despite adopting no such lockdown or masks.[46] As already mentioned, it even emerged

42 Pilita Clark, "Neil Ferguson, a Virus Modeller Sounds the Alarm," *Financial Times*, March 20, 2020, https://www.ft.com/content/7e56cf84-6a9e-11ea-a3c9-1fe-6fedcca75.

43 For a critical discussion of models in general and this one in particular, see Juliette Rouchier and Victorien Barbet, *La diffusion de la Covid-19: que peuvent les modèles?* (Paris: Éditions matériologiques, 2020).

44 Neil Ferguson, "Impact of NPIs," 6–7.

45 Jasmine Gardner, "Intervention Strategies against COVID-19 and Their Estimated Impact on Swedish Healthcare Capacity," *MedRxix* preprint, April 15, 2020, https://www.medrxiv.org/content/10.1101/2020.04.11.20062133v1.full.pdf.

46 See *Our World in Data*, https://ourworldindata.org/explorers/coronavirus-data-explorer?zoomToSelection=true&time=2020-02-03..latest&region=Europe&facet=none&pickerSort=asc&pickerMetric=location&hideControls=true&Metric=Confirmed+deaths&Interval=Cumulative&Relative+to+Population=false&Color+by+test+positivity=false&country=ISR~PSE~FRA~ITA~SVN~BEL~CZE~SVK~HUN~USA~GBR~EuropeanUnion~DEU~AUT~European+Union~OWID_WRL~POL~BIH~BRA~NOR~ESP~PRT~NLD~NZL~JPN~UKR~HKG~CHN~SWE~KEN.

with one of the lowest excess mortalities in Europe for the period 2020-22. At no point in the pandemic was Sweden without lockdown or masks ever experiencing more deaths per capita than the UK with lockdown and masks.

Another critical oversight of the model was its failure to consider the collateral damage inflicted by the lockdown itself. As evidenced by the significant repercussions observed in both Western nations and the developing world which were mentioned above, the societal and economic impacts of lockdowns have been tremendous. This underscores the complexity of pandemic response strategies and highlights the need for a nuanced understanding of the trade-offs involved in implementing interventions.

The Imperial College model also introduced elements of knowledge which were crucial, yet it chose to ignore them: "The WHO China Joint Mission Report suggested that 80% of transmission occurred in the household, although this was in a context where interpersonal contacts were drastically reduced by the interventions put in place."[47] If 80% of the infections occurred at home, what was the point of the lockdown, i.e., of forcibly keeping people at home, in the first place? Let us recall that this report was published already on March 16, 2020.

Neil Ferguson's track record already included a series of apocalyptic predictions that failed to align with reality. In 2002, he forecasted a death toll ranging from 50,000 to 150,000 from BSE (mad cow disease), yet the actual number of deaths was 177.[48] Similarly, he predicted in 2005 a death toll of 200 million from the bird flu, while the actual figure

---

47 Neil Ferguson, "Impact of NPIs," 15.

48 Steerpike, "Six Questions That Neil Ferguson Should Be Asked," *The Spectator*, April 16, 2020, https://www.spectator.co.uk/article/six-questions-that-neil-ferguson-should-be-asked/.

was 282.[49] In 2009, Ferguson's swine flu model projected a reasonable worst-case scenario of 65,000 deaths in the UK and already then recommended school closures. The government opted not to follow this advice, a decision that seems wise given that the actual death toll from swine flu in the UK was 457.[50]

The impact of the Imperial College model in 2020 extended far beyond the specific measures it prompted; it also influenced prevailing attitudes and shaped public health policies across the world. Neil Ferguson and the Scientific Advisory Group for Emergencies (SAGE), which advises the UK government, openly expressed admiration for the "innovative intervention" of the Chinese authorities, particularly the highly authoritarian lockdown implemented in Wuhan and later across China. This contributed to shifting parameters within Western countries, much to Ferguson's own surprise:

> "I think people's sense of what is possible in terms of control changed quite dramatically between January and March," Professor Ferguson says.... "It's a communist one-party state, we said. We couldn't get away with it in Europe, we thought ... and then Italy did it. And we realized we could.... These days, lockdown feels inevitable." It was, he reminds me, anything but. "If China had not done it," he says, "the year would have been very different."[51]

It is interesting that until 1989, the Western liberal left firmly condemned the Iron Curtain and the repression of people who sought to escape communist countries, yet during Covid

49 Steerpike, "Six Questions."

50 Steerpike, "Six Questions."

51 Tom Whipple, "Professor Neil Ferguson: People Don't Agree with Lockdown and Try to Undermine the Scientists," *The Times*, December 25, 2020, https://www.thetimes.co.uk/article/people-don-t-agree-with-lockdown-and-try-to-undermine-the-scientists-gnms7mp98.

it approved of and sought to emulate the Chinese communist regime, which submitted its citizens to an even tighter grip than the one which prevailed during the Cold War. Fear is powerful when skillfully mobilized.

Like Prymula, however, Ferguson failed to live by his own recommendations: he was caught meeting with his lover, who lived in another household with her own family, during the strict lockdown he had advocated. Compounding the situation, Ferguson was at that time still in quarantine after having himself contracted Covid. As the *Telegraph*, which revealed the incident, remarked, "The revelation of the 'illegal' tryst will infuriate millions of couples living apart and banned by the government from meeting up during the lockdown, which is now in its seventh week." Ferguson indeed resigned from SAGE.[52]

Tomas Pueyo, or how a "Silicon Valley entrepreneur" was promoted to expert in epidemiology

Tomas Pueyo's seminal article on Covid, published on the popular blogsite Medium, was a turning point for many, as it brought to light the severity of the pandemic in a way that erased any inclination to trivialize the virus.[53] With over 40 million views, his comprehensive analysis, spanning 6,000 words, depicted the alarming exponential growth of coronavirus cases: "The coronavirus is already here. It's hidden, and it's growing exponentially." Pueyo cited the World Health Organization's reported fatality rate of 3.4% for the virus—

52 Anna Mikhailova, "Exclusive: Government Scientist Neil Ferguson Resigns after Breaking Lockdown Rules to Meet His Married Lover," *The Telegraph*, May 5, 2020, https://www.telegraph.co.uk/news/2020/05/05/exclusive-government-scientist-neil-ferguson-resigns-breaking/.

53 Tomas Pueyo, "Coronavirus: Why You Must Act Now," *Medium.com*, March 10, 2020, https://tomaspueyo.medium.com/coronavirus-act-today-or-people-will-die-f4d3d9cd99ca.

never mind that the actual rate later turned out to be around 0.3%, so Pueyo's was in fact a "vast miscalculation."[54] Worse, Pueyo's "take" was that the fatality rate could potentially reach as high as 6.5% (which is twenty times more than the real rate), particularly in countries "not prepared" to handle the outbreak. Such a fatality rate, he warned, would be "thirty times worse than the flu." However, he thought that "countries that act fast can reduce the number of deaths by a factor of ten."[55]

What might account for such a gross exaggeration is that Pueyo naively accepted the statistics provided by China, according to which the number of cases remained very limited outside of Hubei thanks to the strict lockdown regime which was implemented there,[56] without ever considering the potential for underreporting or manipulation by the Chinese government.

Additionally, Pueyo's projections were based on the mistaken assumption that a significant percentage of Covid-19 cases would require hospitalization and intensive care, as purported, again, by the Chinese data: "Around 20% of cases require hospitalization, 5% of cases require the Intensive Care Unit (ICU), and around 2.5% require very intensive help, with items such as ventilators or ECMO (extra-corporeal oxygenation)."[57] An apocalyptic description of overwhelmed health services in Italy followed, concluding again on the would-be wise terms: "All of this is what drives a system to have a fatality

54 See Ronald B. Brown, "Public Health Lessons Learned from Biases in Coronavirus Mortality Overestimations," *Disaster Medicine and Public Health Preparedness*, August 12, 2020, https://www.ncbi.nlm.nih.gov/pmc/articles/PMC7511835/.

55 Pueyo, "Coronavirus."

56 Raymond Zhong, "No 'Negative' News: How China Censored the Coronavirus," *The New York Times*, December 19, 2020, https://www.nytimes.com/2020/12/19/technology/china-coronavirus-censorship.html.

57 Pueyo, "Coronavirus."

rate of ~4% instead of ~0.5%. If you want your city or your country to be part of the 4%, don't do anything today." Every day of delay in taking these "indispensable measures" was shown as having a catastrophic impact (a 40% increase in the cumulative number of cases).

On March 13, 2020, Pueyo, presented as a "Silicon Valley entrepreneur," was invited on Channel 4 News together with epidemiologist John Edmunds. Edmunds defended the notion that the UK would have to "achieve herd immunity," to which Pueyo theatrically held his head in his hands and exclaimed, "Do we really want 20% or 30% of the population to catch this,... so are we saying we want to kill 200,000 people in the UK? ... We don't want people to catch it, otherwise they're going to die!" He announced that the NHS would collapse in two weeks "if we don't take measures now": "We need to catch this before the weekend!"[58] The fact the Edmunds calmly (and rightly) pointed out that containment was no longer possible could not mitigate the effect of Pueyo's dramatic words: panic became the order of the day.

According to sociologist Warren Pearce, Tomas Pueyo contributed to making experts fashionable again.[59] Curiously, he had never made any claim to being an expert in epidemiology before: "a glance at his Medium profile showed ... a range of posts with titles such as 'What the Rise of Skywalker Can Teach about Storytelling' and 'What I Learned Building a Horoscope That Blew Up on Facebook.' This all seemed like

58 See the Twitter post of Channel 4 News (@Channel4News), "'We need to catch this before the weekend,'" Twitter, March 13, 2020, 10:12 pm, https://twitter.com/Channel4News/status/1238573667002523648, or the whole show on YouTube at Channel 4 News, "Coronavirus: Are We Doing Enough?" YouTube video, 45:13, March 13, 2020, *Channel 4 News*, https://www.youtube.com/watch?v=C98FmoZVbjs.

59 See Warren Pearce, "What Does Covid-19 Mean for Expertise? The Case of Tomas Pueyo," *iHuman* (blog), June 16, 2020, https://www.sheffield.ac.uk/ihuman/blog/what-does-covid-19-mean-expertise-case-tomas-pueyo.

a poor fit for the new age of expert deference that we were supposed to be experiencing."[60] Indeed, he published neither his method nor his code in his Medium post,[61] an absence of falsifiable sources which brings us back to Popper's definition of pseudoscience.

Commenting on Pueyo, Warren Pearce raises the question of what science is, which experts to trust, and how to disentangle science, emotion, and politics.[62] Instead of Pueyo being exposed as the unqualified amateur that he was, it was John Edmunds who appeared again in the media a few months later to now claim that the lockdown delay had indeed "cost a lot of lives."[63] Today, as shown in Chapter 2, we know from the Swedish case and the German inquiry that the lockdown most likely cost many more lives than it saved, i.e., it was never justified in the first place.

Warren Pearce also raises the question of the role of the blogosphere in helping to qualify the claims of would-be experts. Bloggers appeal to the public thanks to their spontaneity and perceived lack of arrogance, which goes to show, he claims, that the notion of expertise should be more inclusive and open to criticism.[64] He shows with the example of the speed at which the Covid cases were supposed to multiply that a misunderstanding had arisen as to the role of epidemiological models vs. advisers—the two are conflated, yet producers of models typically peddle a wider range of possibilities, which allows media to dramatize options: "Role conflation presents a challenge to science advice and highlights the need for a diversity of expertise, a structured process for

60 Pearce, "What Does Covid-19 Mean."

61 Pearce, "What Does Covid-19 Mean."

62 Pearce, "What Does Covid-19 Mean."

63 "Coronavirus: Lockdown Delay 'Cost a Lot of Lives,' Says Science Adviser," *BBC*, June 7, 2020, https://www.bbc.com/news/uk-politics-52955034.

64 Pearce, "What Does Covid-19 Mean."

selecting experts, and greater clarity regarding the methods by which expert consensus is achieved."[65] The media, intent on sensationalizing issues, usually wastes no time on such musings.

Boldly claiming to be a "communications wizard," "spell-caster," and "world-class storyteller," Pueyo later bragged about how much money he made thanks to Covid:

> Soon, it would turn out that my skills were applicable outside of the corporate world. During COVID, my articles were read by hundreds of millions of people. I appeared on TV and in the media around the world. My ideas guided the domestic policy of dozens of countries like Germany, the US, India, Spain, Canada, Singapore, Japan, Bulgaria, Denmark, Finland, the Philippines, Thailand, Sri Lanka, Pakistan, Kuwait, Argentina, Costa Rica. But that was just the beginning. Since then, I've gathered 85,000 people in this newsletter, and now I live off of it. I also have 330k followers on Twitter, with hundreds of millions of impressions every year. The early growth was from COVID, but you can easily tell when I started taking it seriously. And recently, I've been able to replicate this success on YouTube.[66]

Tomas Pueyo might have profited from Covid in a rather insensitive and opportunistic manner in the context of such a global health crisis, but scientific expertise certainly did not come out of it stronger.

---

65 Warren Pearce, "Trouble in the Trough: How Uncertainties Were Downplayed in the UK's Science Advice on Covid-19," *Humanities and Social Sciences Communications* 7, no. 122 (2020), https://doi.org/10.1057/s41599-020-00612-w. Many thanks to the author for providing me with these references.

66 See Tomas Pueyo, "How to Become a Communications Wizard," *Uncharted Territories* (blog), March 14, 2024, https://unchartedterritories.tomaspueyo.com/p/business-communication-course.

When "science" serves to justify the irrationality of panic politics

New York Governor Andrew Cuomo often claimed in his famous daily press briefs in spring 2020, "I wear a mask to protect you" and explained that to wear a mask served to send the message, "I respect you."[67] That this attitude was rather sanctimonious became clear when Cuomo, until then so humane, slammed the New York homeless who slept in the subways at night as "disgusting."[68] He was indignant that they should display such lack of regard for transit workers as to risk contaminating them; on the other hand, he never wondered where else the homeless were supposed to sleep and if their lives were not worth protecting, too. Even more to the point, if the collective prophylactic purpose implied by the mask did not apply to the whole of the population and excluded sections of it as unworthy, it was useless and had to be insincere. But virtue signaling and class recognition were more important than "science."

In the Czech Republic, people had to wear a mask at all times, including when they walked or ran alone in nature.[69] Rumors of drones circling up and verifying the compliance of citizens in woods, fields, and mountains started to circulate. The amusing story of policemen monitoring two nudists on an empty beach and making them mask up made world

67 "Governor Cuomo Urges New Yorkers to Wear Masks," *Reuters*, 12, YouTube video, 1:57, May 13, 2020, https://www.youtube.com/watch?v=Qbtd-piB1Byg.

68 "Cuomo Calls Subway Cars Filled with Homeless People 'Disgusting,'" *The New York Times*, April 28, 2020, https://www.nytimes.com/2020/04/28/nyregion/coronavirus-new-york-update.html.

69 Irena Válová, "Roušky v lese jsou stále povinné. Přes ujišťování politiků to říká opatření ministerstva zdravotnictví," *Česká justice*, April 9, 2020, https://www.ceska-justice.cz/2020/04/rousky-v-lese-jsou-stale-povinne-pres-ujistovani-politiku-to-rika-opatreni-ministerstva-zdravotnictvi/.

headlines.[70] At the time, the Czech Republic had an excellent Covid record, with very few casualties. Was this the proof that masks worked? It is doubtful if we remember that New York Governor Cuomo published figures in early May 2020, after weeks of lockdown and much publicity given to wearing masks, according to which 66% of new hospitalizations in New York occurred amongst people who had stayed at home,[71] or alternatively, as Tomas Pueyo reported, that 80% of the infections occurred at home in China.

But at the game of purity, someone always plays better. Czech authorities could reproach Governor Cuomo that in New York, children didn't have to wear masks, whereas the more careful Czech children had to be masked from birth onwards. At least it was so for the first two weeks of lockdown, then the lower limit was raised at the end of March 2020 to two years of age.[72] Czech authorities doubtless thought Governor Cuomo was irresponsible to let three-year-old children walk around without masks—and despaired Czech parents, who risked an €800 fine if their toddlers didn't comply. In Spain and Italy, authorities deemed both Cuomo and the Czechs irresponsible to let people walk outside at all. Their citizens were strictly confined at home, the only exception being to buy food. Children did not go out of their homes at all for three weeks in Italy and seven weeks straight in Spain.[73]

---

70 Barry Neild, "Czech Nudists Told to Wear Face Masks by Police," *CNN*, April 10, 2020, https://edition.cnn.com/travel/article/czech-nudists-virus-police/index.html.

71 Noah Higgins-Dunn and Kevin Breuninger, "Cuomo Says It's 'Shocking' Most New Coronavirus Hospitalizations Are People Who Had Been Staying Home," *CNBC*, May 6, 2020, https://www.cnbc.com/2020/05/06/ny-gov-cuomo-says-its-shocking-most-new-coronavirus-hospitalizations-are-people-staying-home.html.

72 Pavel Cechl, "Konečně. Ministerstvo řeklo, zda roušky musejí mít děti a kojenci," *Deník.cz*, March 30, 2020, https://www.denik.cz/z_domova/povinne-rousky-deti-cesko.html.

73 Mireia Orgiles et. al., "Psychological Symptoms in Italian, Spanish and Portuguese Youth during the COVID-19 Crisis: A Longitudinal Study," *Child*

In France, McKinsey designed an administrative authorization that people had to print at home, fill out, and sign, granting themselves the authorization to go out (outside of work) for one hour maximum, in a one-kilometer perimeter maximum, with one child maximum.[74] Meanwhile, in Austria, the mask was not compulsory for the first six weeks, then compulsory only for indoor shopping, while people were free to walk outside without.[75] In Germany, the Deutsche Bahn company made passengers wear FF2 masks, but the staff had to wear only surgical masks.[76]

Where is the scientific logic in all this? And if the mask was so important, why were authorities repeatedly caught posing with their mask for the camera and taking it off as soon as they thought the camera was off?[77]

In the Czech Republic, fathers were forbidden from attending the birth of their children on the pretext that their presence posed an infection risk to the hospital personnel. This was criticized by a Czech journalist as a measure tailored to "cost nothing while looking like the government is doing something."[78] In France, fathers were allowed to come for the delivery but had to leave the hospital two hours after the

---

Psychiatry & Human Development, June 26, 2021, https://link.springer.com/article/10.1007/s10578-021-01211-9.

74 Nicolas Monnet, "Confinement: 1 kilomètre pour marcher autour de chez soi, ça correspond à quoi?" *L'indépendant*, March 27, 2020, https://www.lindependant.fr/2020/03/27/confinement-1-kilometre-autour-de-chez-soi-ca-correspond-a-quoi,8821248.php.

75 "Covid-19 pandemic in Austria," Wikipedia, https://en.wikipedia.org/wiki/COVID-19_pandemic_in_Austria.

76 See Anthony LaMesa (@ajLamesa), "The Science," Twitter, October 7, 2022, 2:56 pm, https://twitter.com/ajlamesa/status/1771700651275227433.

77 See, for instance, here: Ancient Man, "Global Leaders at G20 Remove Masks after Posing for Photos!" YouTube video, 0:08, November 1, 2021, https://www.youtube.com/watch?v=5AqIEwc2C8c.

78 Petr Bittner, "Připravit otce o porod je to nejhorší, s čím vláda přišla," *Deník referendum*, March 30, 2020, https://denikreferendum.cz/clanek/30979-pripravit-otce-o-porod-je-to-nejhorsi-s-cim-vlada-prisla.

birth and not come back, or else stay confined in the room with mother and baby and not go out for the duration of the stay (usually a few days). A similar measure was implemented in the state of New York but was rapidly revised in view of the outcry it provoked.[79] Who was right? In the ranking of Covid deaths per capita, the Czech Republic ended up in a worse position than the US, which ended up in a significantly worse position than France.[80] Among 21,027 women questioned in 12 countries of Europe, 62% "were not allowed their companion of choice" during labor in 2020-21.[81] In many countries, women were additionally forced to wear a mask throughout their entire labor.

In Slovakia, a mother who gave birth while positive for Covid was allowed to see her child for the first time after twelve days.[82] In the UK, a mother was kept apart from her dying newborn son because she had Covid.[83] As daycare

---

79 Holly Yan and Kristina Sgueglia, "New York State Overrules a Hospital Policy Saying Mothers Must Give Birth without Their Partners," *CNN*, March 29, 2020, https://edition.cnn.com/2020/03/29/health/new-york-hospital-childbirth-policy-overturned/index.html.

80 See the tracking website Our World in Data: https://ourworldindata.org/explorers/coronavirus-data-explorer?zoomToSelection=true&time=2020-02-03..latest&region=Europe&facet=none&country=ISR~PSE~FRA~ITA~SVN~BEL~CZE~SVK~HUN~USA~GBR~EuropeanUnion~DEU~AUT~European+Union~OWID_WRL~POL~BIH~BRA~NOR~ESP~PRT~NLD~NZL~JPN~UKR~HKG~CHN~SWE&pickerSort=asc&pickerMetric=location&hideControls=true&Interval=Cumulative&Relative+to+Population=true&Color+by+test+positivity=false&Metric=Confirmed+deaths.

81 Marzia Lazzerini et.al., "Quality of Facility-Based Maternal and Newborn Care around the Time of Childbirth during the COVID-19 Pandemic: Online Survey Investigating Maternal Perspectives in 12 Countries of the WHO European Region," *The Lancet*, December 24, 2021, https://www.thelancet.com/journals/lanepe/article/PIIS2666-7762(21)00254-4/fulltext.

82 Denisa Gdovinová, "Žena rodila s koronavírusom a svoje dieťa uvidela až po dvanástich dňoch. Neizolujte matky od detí, vyzývajú odborníci," *Denník N*, October 30, 2020, https://dennikn.sk/2113967/zena-rodila-s-koronavirusom-a-svoje-dieta-uvidela-az-po-dvanastich-dnoch-neizolujte-matky-od-deti-vyzyvaju-odbornici/.

83 Neil Johnston, "NHS Staff Kept Mother with Covid Apart from Dying Newborn

centers and kindergartens reopened in Europe in late spring 2020, toddlers and young children were confronted with masked caretakers, a potentially terrifying sight for them. As they could not see their lips, psychologists warned they would be retarded in their speech development, which is exactly what happened.[84]

In European countries with mask mandates, the populations were told that to wear the mask was necessary primarily in case they sneezed or coughed. So in spring, allergy season, they were expected to sneeze into their masks—and then what? Have their faces covered in snot? Was it not more probable that people would remove their masks to sneeze into a paper tissue before replacing the mask? If so, what was the point of the mask? And what to do with the numerous people who wore the mask on their chins? Should militia men wearing gas masks remain on standby in every subway carriage, ready to neutralize recalcitrants?

The Czech Republic was the first European country to make masks compulsory, but masks were unavailable, so people rediscovered a DIY nostalgia for communist times and made their own cloth masks. Hygienic issues stemmed from such usage. As people wore the same cloth mask for days or weeks on end, they rapidly smelled bad. When restaurants reopened but the masks were still compulsory, people raised their masks, ate or drunk, and then put them back down over their mouths, so the masks now doubled as napkins. Prime Minister Andrej Babiš nevertheless boasted in a tweet addressed to President Trump on March 29, 2020: "@realDonaldTump, try tackling virus the Czech way. Wearing a simple

Son," *The Telegraph*, September 11, 2024, https://www.telegraph.co.uk/news/2024/09/11/nhs-covid-inquiry-dying-baby-catherine-todd-ulster/.

84 Vanessa Clarke, "How Did the Pandemic Impact Babies Starting School As Children Now?," *BBC*, September 1, 2024, https://www.bbc.com/news/articles/c39kry9j3rno.

cloth mask, decreases the speed of the virus by 80%! Czech Republic has made it OBLIGATORY for its citizens to wear a mask in the public. Pls retweet. God bless America!"[85] By May 1, 2020, the Czech Republic indeed identified only 257 Covid deaths (compared, for instance, to 2,719 in similarly populated Sweden). But by November 17, 2020, the Czech Republic had 6,416 Covid deaths, i.e., more than the 6,344 Swedish ones. By August 2021, Czechia had one of the worst confirmed death rate in the world despite its "Germanic genes" and its home-made masks.

Before the country became "best in Covid," as the Czechs bitterly laughed, health authorities had randomly tested 27,000 people in spring 2020 and discovered that only about 100 people had been in contact with the virus. Covid was simply not present in the country: by sheer good luck, there were very few clusters of people who had traveled to the Czech Republic from infected areas before the borders were sealed at the same pace as the rest of Europe. Austria reached similar conclusions: less than 1% of the population had encountered the virus.

Vít Klusák and Marika Pecháčková shot a moving documentary film on the mobilization of Czech society during this first, rather stupefying, lockdown. The film is evocatively entitled *Velké nic* (The Great Nothing).[86] Apart from the stunning beauty of empty Prague streets shot with exceptionally good cameras not normally used in a documentary film but which were cheap to rent at a time when the film industry was on standby, the film depicts the dedication of Czech women,

85 See Andrej Babiš (@AndrejBabis), "Mr. President @realDonaldTrump, try tackling virus the Czech way," Twitter, March 29, 2020, 8:19 am, https://twitter.com/AndrejBabis/status/1244147274298654720.

86 See Ian Willoughby, "'It Was Very Visual: New Doc Revisits Covid Period in Czechia," *Radio Prague International*, March 14, 2023, https://english.raio.cz/it-was-very-visual-new-doc-revisits-covid-period-czechia-8777565.

who sat down and sewed home-made masks in order to "help" those who might be in need of them, especially health personnel. As one of them put it, while herself unwittingly wearing her mask under her nose, these women did not volunteer their time to help the government or "the system" but to "save the people." Another one explained that she "had to do something." The mask was a "symbol" of "something positive": "That the mask works or doesn't work is completely equal," she concluded.[87]

To question the ethics of the measures was to snap Harry Potter's wand in two

Many citizens around the world opened their windows at the given hour every day or week to cheer health workers.[88] Who would not applaud the selflessness of frontline workers, especially nurses and doctors? The answer is, those who had health personnel living in their building and who wrote anonymous letters of threat and denunciation or expelled them for "selfishly exposing them" to the virus: such stories appeared in all countries.[89] Many people normally treat ordinary small workers with little or no consideration but applauded "frontline workers" all the louder that they stayed home while they let these small people do the risky job outdoors. How much consideration would these people still get once the crisis was over? The answer was made clear soon enough: nurses

87 Vít Klusák and Marika Pecháčková, *Velké nic*, 2020, https://www.csfd.cz/film/1246875-velke-nic/prehled/.

88 Luke Hurst, "Coronavirus: Health Workers Clapped across the World for Battling on the COVID-19 Frontline," *EuroNews*, March 24, 2020, https://www.euronews.com/2020/03/24/coronavirus-health-workers-clapped-across-the-world-for-battling-on-the-covid-19-frontline.

89 Kirk Semple, "'Afraid to Be a Nurse': Health Workers under Attack," *The New York Times*, April 27, 2020, https://www.nytimes.com/2020/04/27/world/americas/coronavirus-health-workers-attacked.html.

and physicians, so praised one year earlier, were ruthlessly dismissed and vilified if they refused to take the new Covid vaccine in 2021,[90] including Professors Martin Kulldorff (Harvard) and Aaron Kheriaty (Irvine), both because they just had Covid and pleaded natural immunity. Ethics professor Julie Ponesse was also fired from Western University (Canada) because she, logically, refused the vaccine mandate for ethical reasons.[91]

People were not shy about lecturing others, either. A French sports journalist caught Covid and nearly died. He gave a vibrant testimony as to the suffering he endured, the health consequences, the devotion of the hospital team who saved him, and his sheer luck to even survive. He ended by lecturing to those irresponsible people who didn't take the virus seriously and flouted the lockdown. Hand on heart, in the name of all the people who were risking their lives to save ours, the least we could do for them, he said, was to follow the rules and not endanger them.[92] This was a touching testimony, but less touching are the circumstances in which this journalist caught the virus himself: by going to Northern Italy to watch a Juventus FC football match at a time when the pandemic had already started. Going to a football match with 80,000 spectators in a contaminated area did not prevent him from feeling entitled to lecture others on proper behavior.

---

90 Carlie Porterfield and Lisa Kim, "Hospitals Begin Firing Staffers Who Refuse Covid Vaccines—Leading Some to Fear Staffing Shortages," *Forbes*, September 27, 2021, https://www.forbes.com/sites/carlieporterfield/2021/09/27/hospitals-begin-firing-staffers-who-refuse-covid-vaccines---leading-some-to-fear-staffing-shortages/?sh=f8ca5b35f9e4.

91 See Julie Ponesse, *My Choice: The Ethical Case Against Covid-19 Vaccine Mandates* (Toronto: The Democracy Fund, 2020).

92 Vincent Duluc, "Vincent Duluc, touché par le coronavirus: 'Tu prends une grande claque,'" *L'Équipe*, May 1, 2020, https://www.lequipe.fr/Football/Actualites/Vincent-duluc-touche-par-le-coronavirus-tu-prends-une-grande-claque/1131307.

French trade unions were worried about people going back to work and "risking their lives,"[93] but they were equally fiercely against the government preventing them from taking their summer holiday by keeping beaches closed. In France, it was too dangerous to work but not too dangerous to cross the country by train to lie on the beach for a much-needed respite.[94]

Breath is death

"Breath is death," an Orwell-inspired motto which circulated on social media, aptly characterizes the atmosphere in the Western world as the Covid pandemic broke out. To terrify people into believing that only the mask could save them from Covid and from almost certain death has not remained without consequences. Social media abounds to this day with postings from individuals who wear increasingly complex contraptions, convinced they can survive their outings in public only thanks to them. As Lachlan Blake, a Twitter user from Australia, put it, after such social conditioning, these ordinary people are "suffering from a hyperinflated fear of becoming critically ill and have made pathological changes to the way they socialize in order to cope with this new phobia." Again, inducing and using fear of contaminated air is nothing new in biopolitical governmentality. The Czechs who are old enough remember having to wear gas masks in the 1980s to

---

93 Raphaëlle Besse Desmoulières, "Coronavirus: les syndicats veulent protéger les salariés obligés d'aller travailler," *Le Monde*, March 20, 2020, https://www.lemonde.fr/politique/article/2020/03/20/coronavirus-les-syndicats-veulent-proteger-les-salaries-obliges-d-aller-travailler_6033791_823448.html.

94 Pauline Rouquette, "Pourquoi les vacances de l'été 2020 seront historiques," *Europé 1*, July 4, 2020, https://www.europe1.fr/societe/vacances-post-coronavirus-des-vacances-historiques-et-exceptionnelles-selon-un-Bresociologue-3979223.

train against the biological or chemical warfare that the West was going to launch "any time soon."

A video of the same Lachlan Blake garnered 700,000 views on Facebook in 2021. It showed him being handcuffed, age 17, by Australian police for refusing to tell his name and address—unless the real cause of his arrest was his calm, amusing lecture to the police on his own civil rights, which visibly irked the officers dealing with him.[95] He was prompted to show his ID because he was not wearing a mask outdoors at an anti-lockdown protest and was subject to control if he was within the ten-kilometer radius from his home in which Australians were allowed to travel in the frame of the lockdown. Ten minutes after this spectacular arrest, he was released on the reasoning that he had been drinking a coffee, so he hadn't needed to mask after all—this was "science."

Summary of Chapter 3

Chapter 3 showed that during Covid, the instrumentalization of science and expertise was evident in various ways, including the use of financial incentives to shape public health messaging and the close ties between regulatory agencies and the pharmaceutical industry. This raises concerns about conflicts of interest and the neutrality of the narrative surrounding Covid and the vaccination efforts. Mainstream media's role in amplifying this narrative, often without questioning the underlying motivations or potential biases of consulted experts, further compounded these issues. This absence of critical thinking highlights the need for greater scrutiny and transparency at the intersection of science, public health, and industry interests. The story of three particular influencers

95 See MCJ Report, "Lachlan Blake converses with police," Facebook, June 12, 2021, https://www.facebook.com/watch/?v=250273656874105.

of the pandemic illustrated the hubris, exaggerations, and opportunistic motives in public health expertise. The pandemic response in various countries was marked by multiple inconsistencies and controversies, leading us to relativize the notion of "science."

Chapter 4

A reckoning about the Covid measures is necessary and urgent

> Humanity's capacity for justice makes democracy possible, but humanity's inclination to injustice makes democracy necessary.
>
> Stefan Zweig, *The World of Yesterday*

To play with democratic values and habituate public opinion to authoritarian measures was to start a ride down a slippery slope. A reckoning of the Covid policy failures is all the more necessary and urgent that the censorship and control tools adopted on the pretext of Covid are still in place and remain at the disposal of all governments; in many cases, they have been further strengthened *after* Covid.

During Covid: How even democracies can be repressive

The Covid responses varied considerably from country to country, which shows yet again that "science," in this case medicine, is largely cultural and political. The crisis provided both autocracies and democracies with an unexpected biopolitical opportunity to grab ever more power.[1] It also reaffirmed an old European stereotype according to which southern

1 Selam Gebrekidan, "For Autocrats, and Others, Coronavirus Is a Chance to Grab Even More Power," *The New York Times*, March 30, 2020, https://www.nytimes.com/2020/03/30/world/europe/coronavirus-governments-power.html.

countries are more authoritarian and less efficient than northern countries. Only five countries in Europe: France, Italy, Spain, Cyprus, and Greece submitted their populations to strict rules about coming out of their houses with a certificate or safe conduct tightly controlled by the police. Meanwhile, Sweden, Finland, Denmark, Norway, and the Netherlands let their populations go out freely.[2] The variety of the responses to Covid documents not "science," but a socio-political difference between countries in their attitude toward their populations, from trusting them to considering them with systematic suspicion.

Even more police powers were conferred to the police by French regional and local authorities than by the national ones; numerous curfews were implemented and duly monitored. Access to recreational or green spaces was restricted with arguments such as "Lockdown is no vacation!" while in other places it was forbidden to buy only one baguette or one newspaper at a time, or to sit on a public bench, or in yet other places, to sit on a bench for more than two minutes.[3] According to sociologists Nicolas Mariot and Théo Boulakia:

> The difference in reaction is clearly linked to the coercive habits of governments: we show that the more police officers per capita in European states, the more accustomed they are to suspending civic liberties, the more they locked their populations down. During this pandemic, we have therefore witnessed the resurgence of old habits relying on the punitive management of the population.[4]

---

2 Marina Julienne, "Covid-19: le bilan d'une surveillance massive," *CNRS Le journal*, April 10, 2024, https://lejournal.cnrs.fr/articles/covid-19-bilan-du-ne-surveillance-massive.

3 Julienne, "Covid-19."

4 Julienne, "Covid-19." See also their volume: Théo Boulakia, Nicolas Mariot, *L'attestation: Une experience d'obéissance de masse, printemps 2020* (Paris: Anamosa, 2023).

In fact, the striking point about the lockdown is that it was more about enforcing submission to authority than about health.[5] The French population (67 million) was submitted to 21 million police controls between March 17, 2020, and May 11, 2020. Spain meted out 2,157 fines per 100,000 inhabitants, France 1,630, and Italy 709, while at the other end of the scale, the Netherlands issued 77 fines per 100,000 inhabitants.[6] The French case also shows that those social classes of the population that were already the most dominated were the most compliant: women, the poor, and the less politicized.[7] Only about a third of the population attempted to circumvent the new, authoritarian rules. The data at the basis of Théo Boulakia and Nicolas Mariot's volume *L'attestation* (The Certificate) is publicly accessible, and the volume's website documents the stringency of the French police during the pandemic.[8] At least the Spanish top court ruled the lockdown unconstitutional and returned the 1.1 million fines the police had meted out between March 14, 2020, and June 21, 2020[9]—a piece of news that conspicuously failed to make big headlines in the *New York Times* or the *Guardian*. Britain also meted out 27,600 court convictions for breach of Covid rules, including 4,000 since all restrictions were lifted in 2022.[10]

---

5 Laurent Mucchielli, "Le confinement de 2020 en France: une expérience de soumission à l'autorité," *Quartier général*, May 24, 2024, https://qg.media/blog/laurent-mucchielli/le-confinement-de-2020-en-france-une-experience-de-soumission-a-lautorite/.

6 Mucchielli, "Le confinement de 2020 en France."

7 Mucchielli, "Le confinement de 2020 en France."

8 See https://l-attestation.github.io/films.html.

9 AP, "Spanish Government Returns Fines for Breaking Virus Lockdown Rules," October 22, 2021, https://apnews.com/article/coronavirus-pandemic-europe-health-spain-59be7c26d2a76255119743f23541d310.

10 Alistair Gray and Clara Murray, "Nearly 4,000 Convicted of Covid Rule Breaches in England since Curbs Ended," *Financial Times*, May 22, 2024, https://www.ft.com/content/84dad3e3-cbe2-4dcb-a318-3456d9d64e3e.

Chile sent its army against protesters, and Bolivia postponed elections. Britain granted new "eye-watering" powers to its government to detain people and close borders. As one account noted at the time, "leaders across the globe are invoking executive powers and seizing virtually dictatorial authority with scant resistance," since "extraordinary times call for extraordinary measures."[11] Police across the world were "given license to control behavior in a way that would normally be extreme even for an authoritarian state."[12] "Grueling and humiliating punishments" were often enforced on the "poorest and most vulnerable groups," including "tens of millions who live hand-to-mouth and risk starving if they do not defy lockdowns and seek work."[13]

Migrant workers in India were sprayed with bleach at the risk of damaging their health as a supposed means to "disinfect them"; in Punjab, "people accused of breaking quarantine rules were made to do squats while chanting: 'We are enemies of society. We cannot sit at home.'" "Similarly humiliating tactics" were used in Paraguay, even though to stay in lockdown there was synonymous with dying of hunger; as for the Philippines, "police and local officials trapped curfew violators in dog cages, while others were forced to sit in the midday sun as punishment."[14] In Hungary, measures including jail terms were passed for "spreading misinformation" and allowed the nationalist prime minister, Viktor Orbán, to "rule by decree under a state of emergency that has no clear time limit."[15]

---

11 Gray and Murray, "Nearly 4,000 Convicted of Covid Rule Breaches."

12 Rebecca Ratcliffe, "Teargas, Beatings, and Bleach: The Most Extreme Covid-19 Lockdown Control around the World," *The Guardian*, April 1, 2020, https://www.theguardian.com/global-development/2020/apr/01/extreme-coronavirus-lockdown-controls-raise-fears-for-worlds-poorest.

13 Ratcliffe, "Teargas, Beatings, and Bleach."

14 Ratcliffe, "Teargas, Beatings, and Bleach."

15 Ratcliffe, "Teargas, Beatings, and Bleach."

In Israel, authorities used tools normally reserved for counterterrorism, such as tapping into cellphone data to geolocate citizens redefined as "patients," who might have crossed paths with actual, known Covid patients.[16] This is little different from the breaches of citizens' privacy that have been in force in China. The issue at stake is the definition of the healthcare "needs" of the population. Does the close surveillance of our bodies amount to care or to control? Where does "saving lives" stop and intruding into our privacy begin?

Prime Minister Netanyahu insisted that Israel was a democracy: "We have to maintain the balance between the rights of the individual and the needs of general society, and we are doing that."[17] But these measures rather betrayed the presence of an authoritarian mindset: "Mr. Netanyahu's caretaker government on Sunday authorized prison sentences of up to six months for anyone breaching isolation orders; barring visitors, including lawyers, from prison and detention facilities and allowing the police to break up gatherings—as of now, more than 10 people—by means including 'the use of reasonable force.'"[18] The Covid pandemic was used to bring about the further militarization of society:

> The Shin Bet security service was recruited to operate electronic surveillance devices to track patients and their relatives, the Mossad was sent to bring medical equipment, the National Security Council has set up a war room, the Israel Defense Forces Home Front is publicizing recommendations for proper parenting, and above all of them sits Defense Minister Naftali Bennett, who is trying to wrest control of the crisis from the Health Ministry.[19]

---

16 David M. Halbfinger, Isabel Kershner, and Ronen Bergman, "To Track Coronavirus, Israel Moves to Tap Secret Trove of Cellphone Data," *The New York Times*, March 16, 2020, https://www.nytimes.com/2020/03/16/world/middleeast/israel-coronavirus-cellphone-tracking.html.

17 Halbfinger, Kershner, and Bergman, "To Track Coronavirus."

18 Halbfinger, Kershner, and Bergman, "To Track Coronavirus."

19 Ring, "The Militarization of the Coronavirus."

The involvement of law-enforcement agencies in maintaining public health is rarely a good sign for civil rights. One particularly worrisome aspect is the pact established between companies specializing in surveillance and the military. If such a relationship is long attested in the US, it is still a relatively novel phenomenon in Europe. The ARTE film *Seven Billion Suspects* mentioned in Chapter 1 interviewed an English researcher, Chris Jones, who dissected European Council reports. Projects in security matters from the 2010s worth 1.4 billion euros attributed 40% of these funds to private companies: "You can see that the security research program was very heavily influenced by corporate interests. They had a big hand in shaping the program, in how it works, and in setting the priorities by having seats on the advisory groups that determine the work programs."[20]

"To measure the private companies' influence" in matters of digital surveillance, continues the film, it is enough to study the CV of the experts in charge of advising the European Council on matters of security. Out of the twenty experts, "a third admit having ties to firms or lobbies in the security industry."[21] The group's president, Alberto Benedictis, "was even head of the ASD (Aerospace and Defense Industries), the main lobby for defense industries."[22]

As Chris Jones states it, these individuals are not necessarily ill-intentioned, "but there's a saying, 'The road to hell is paved with good intentions.'"[23] As mentioned in Chapter 3, a similar pattern of corporate interests taking over the European Medicines Agency and the American National Institutes of Health is clearly distinguishable, but mainstream media have

20 Louvet, *Tous surveillés*.
21 Louvet, *Tous surveillés*.
22 Louvet, *Tous surveillés*.
23 Louvet, *Tous surveillés*.

not really investigated this unhealthy relationship either. Again, the reason for this lack of interest is prosaic: it would amount to criticizing the vaccine, which is taboo.

After Covid: A few examples of countries implementing ever tougher speech laws

Western democracies seem engaged in a fierce competition since Covid as to who will implement the most repressive measures targeting free speech.

In Scotland, the new Hate Crime and Public Order Act is so drastic in its provision for criminalizing any speech, even held in the privacy of one's home, that it might be construed as "stirring up hatred,"[24] and even the *Guardian* fears it will stifle "honestly expressed, contentious views" and will "stymie public debate."[25] The *Telegraph* claimed more brusquely that the new law had turned Scotland into a "nation of snitches,"[26] a formulation which has the merit of pointing to the direct line between a behavior purposely nudged during Covid and the new normal—or rather, the new abnormal, as pointed out by Aaron Kheriaty.[27]

In Germany, the Minister of Interior claimed in an interview to the *Frankfurter Allgemeine Zeitung* in 2024 that "freedom of expression is not a license for the enemies of the

---

24 Simon Jenkins, "Scotland's Hate Crime Law May Be Well Intentioned, but the Police Should Not Stymie Public Debate," *The Guardian*, April 1, 2024, https://www.theguardian.com/commentisfree/2024/apr/01/scotland-hate-crime-law-public-debate.

25 Jenkins, "Scotland's Hate Crime Law."

26 Allison Pearson, "Yousaf's Laws Have Turned Scotland into a Nation of Snitches—Stalin Would Be Proud," *The Telegraph*, April 2, 2024, https://www.telegraph.co.uk/columnists/2024/04/02/allison-pearson-farce-is-hot-on-the-heels-of-tragedy/.

27 Aaron Kheriaty, *The New Abnormal: The Rise of the Biomedical Security State* (Washington DC: Regnery, 2022).

constitution,"[28] a headline which would not have been out of place in the Germany of the 1930s.

Ireland, Poland, and Canada are also pushing for speech punishment laws:

> The new Irish Taoiseach, Simon Harris, is determined to railroad through the Criminal Justice (Incitement to Violence or Hatred and Hate Offences) Bill, Donald Tusk's government in Poland wants to introduce a new law that would make it a criminal offence to "defame" a member of the LGBT community, and Justin Trudeau is pressing ahead with an Online Harms Bill that makes our own Online Safety Act seem like the First Amendment. It's as if all these "liberal" leaders are saying: "You think Humza Yousaf is the West's foremost opponent of free speech? Hold my beer."[29]

Canada is indeed also planning a drastic law to crack down on social media and make them "safer" from "speech crimes": the Online Harms Act. Canada was marked by protests in Ottawa in winter 2022, the so-called Freedom Convoy, led by truck drivers who opposed the Canadian Covid vaccine mandate and restrictions and whose bank accounts were frozen, an unprecedented measure taken by the Trudeau government as it invoked emergency powers.[30] A Canadian judge later ruled that the use of the Emergencies Act was "unreasonable" and "unconstitutional."[31] Yet, the new law, proposed by the Liberal Party (which

28 Thomas Haldenwang, "Die Meinungsfreiheit ist kein Freibrief für Verfassungsfeinde," *Frankfurter Allgemeine Zeitung*, April 1, 2024, https://www.faz.net/aktuell/politik/inland/verfassungsschutz-thomas-haldenwang-verteidigt-sich-gegen-kritik-19623960.html.

29 Toby Young, "Even Orwell's Thought Police Didn't Go as Far as Trudeau," *The Spectator*, April 20, 2024, https://www.spectator.co.uk/article/even-orwells-thought-police-didnt-go-as-far-as-trudeau/.

30 AP, "Justin Trudeau Invokes Emergency Powers to Quell Trucker Protests in Canada," February 14, 2022, https://www.nbcnews.com/news/world/justin-trudeau-invokes-emergency-powers-quell-trucker-protests-canada-rcna16213.

31 AP, "Judge: Canada's Use of Emergencies Act to Quell Truckers' COVID

goes to show that the notion of liberalism is relative), would raise the maximum penalty from the current five years to life in prison for genocide advocacy online. Judges would also be empowered to sentence citizens to house arrest and/or a fine if there were "reasonable grounds to believe a defendant 'will commit' an offense."[32] The author of the dystopian novel *The Handmaid's Tale*, Margaret Atwood, called the bill "Orwellian" and akin to the "Lettres de cachet all over again."[33]

Moreover, the Canadian law proposal aims to be retroactive, which goes against two principles that govern Western legal tradition, "nullum crimem sine lege" and "nulla poena sine lege": no crime without a law and no punishment without a law. Only one well-known exception has been made (and even so, it was controversial): it was the appearance of the "crime against humanity" legal category in the London Charter of August 1945, a provision that paved the legal pathway for the International Military Tribunal in Nuremberg to judge Nazi criminals. "Crime against humanity" and "genocide" were mobilized post hoc only because the crimes committed by the Nazis, first and foremost the Holocaust, did not infringe Nazi law, yet it was absolutely necessary to punish them. To apply retroactive punishment to criticism in peacetime, on the other hand, is simply unheard of in Western democracies.

Since 2023, the French Parliament has also been considering a law to crack down on "sectarian drift" and "gravely damaging moral ascendency," into which it includes "health gurus who propagate their influence by recommending on

---

Protests Was Unreasonable," *Voice of America*, January 23, 2024, https://www.voanews.com/a/judge-canada-s-use-of-emergencies-act-to-quell-truckers-covid-protests-was-unreasonable-/7452237.html.

32 Marie Woolf, "Margaret Atwood Calls Online Harms Bill 'Orwellian,' Notes Potential for Abuse," *The Globe and Mail*, March 11, 2024, https://www.theglobeandmail.com/politics/article-margaret-atwood-online-harms-bill/.

33 Woolf, "Margaret Atwood."

social media practices and behaviors that are often gravely damaging to people."[34] This vague offense, if adopted as it stands, could lead to serious infringements of freedom of speech in France. Its real purpose is to target a microbiologist and professor of medicine, Didier Raoult, who before Covid had an international reputation but claimed in March-April 2020 in the hospital he was the head of to have found a cure against Covid combining antibiotics with hydroxychloroquine. Raoult achieved global fame after President Trump touted his cure,[35] but he has remained a highly controversial figure and one whom French authorities have relentlessly attempted to silence and ridicule ever since.[36]

Under the premises of the new French law, someone as moderate as Anders Tegnell, who implemented a policy which the vast majority of the West vituperatively disagreed with, might well be considered a criminal threat to public order. Yet again, I have to repeat that much to the chagrin of lockdown supporters, Sweden ended up with one of the lowest excess death rates of Europe in the Covid period.[37]

The French government built on the unprecedented Covid measures to reactivate the obligation to show a special QR

---

34 Conseil d'État, "Avis sur un projet de loi visant à renforcer la lutte contre les dérives sectaires et la répression des emprises mentales gravement dommageables," *conseil-etat.fr*, November 17, 2023, https://www.conseil-etat.fr/avis-consultatifs/derniers-avis-rendus/au-gouvernement/avis-sur-un-projet-de-loi-visant-a-renforcer-la-lutte-contre-les-derives-sectaires-et-la-repression-des-emprises-mentales-gravement-dommageables.

35 Scott Sayare, "He Was a Science Star. Then He Promoted a Questionable Cure for Covid-19," *The New York Times*, May 12, 2020, https://www.nytimes.com/2020/05/12/magazine/didier-raoult-hydroxychloroquine.html.

36 See L.C., "Véran se paie Raoult, 'le charlatan de la Canebière,' pour son retour à l'Assemblée nationale," *Egora*, February 15, 2024, https://www.egora.fr/actus-pro/politiques/veran-se-paie-raoult-le-charlatan-de-la-canebiere-pour-son-retour-lassemblee.

37 According to Statistics Sweden, see Bergstedt, "Anders Tegnell" (see the discussion of Swedish figures in Chapter 1). https://www.svd.se/a/JQvVnj/anders-tegnell-efter-pandemin-overdodlighet-ger-inte-hela-svaret.

code to move around Paris during the summer 2024 Olympic Games,[38] a method of control of movement typical of China. President Macron also threatened to cut off all social media during street riots.[39]

The fight against so-called Covid "fake news" or "disinformation" has effectively weaponized governments against legitimate criticism. Covid seen as a biopolitical case illustrates how easy it has been for authorities to label any dissent as a "terrorist threat" or a "public health threat," just like communist regimes did in the past on a routine basis. Communist history indeed exemplifies how precarious the line between preventing crime and exerting dictatorial rule can be. The current trend in Western democracies to legally criminalize legitimate speech is setting a dangerous precedent and raises the possibility of sanctioning mere thoughts or speech expressed only in private. The potential for abuse is overwhelming.

This movement is all the more indefensible that the official Covid narrative is now proving to have been wrong in many crucial aspects.

The reckoning with freedom-depriving and inefficient Covid measures has begun

"We were wrong, but we didn't know" as a justification for the lockdowns is factually wrong. On March 23, 2020, the Yale School of Public Health unambiguously showed that young

38 "Paris 2024: des QR codes pour circuler aux abords des sites olympiques," *France Info*, November 29, 2023, https://www.francetvinfo.fr/les-jeux-olympiques/paris-2024/paris-2024-des-qr-codes-pour-circuler-aux-abords-des-sites-olympiques_6213372.html.

39 Kim Willsher, "Macron Accused of Authoritarianism after Threat to Cut off Social Media," *The Guardian*, July 5, 2023, https://www.theguardian.com/world/2023/jul/05/french-government-should-control-social-media-during-unrest-macron-says.

children were at less than 0.01% risk (fatality rate) of dying from Covid, while those above 80 had a risk thought to be of at least 15%, possibly as high as 22%.[40] Citing Imperial College London data published on March 16, 2020, the BBC and many other media confirmed that the chance of dying from Covid lay between 0.5% and 1% (the real rate would prove to be 0.3%), with almost zero risk for children and the highest risk for people over 80.[41]

"We were wrong, but we didn't know" is a fallacious defense also because it was underpinned by censorship, a censorship championed and enforced by the very same authorities now feigning ignorance. As the official narrative gradually unravels, each domino of the dogma falls in succession, prompting the authorities responsible for the Covid measures to scramble and evade accountability—but only rarely to admit they were wrong.

Neil Ferguson, the author of the famous Imperial College model that predicted millions of deaths without a lockdown, has denied ever urging for a lockdown.[42] Devi Sridhar, one of the most prominent public health voices in the UK who argued for a strict lockdown, has blamed "ministers" for "what went wrong with Covid" while exonerating "scientists" such as herself from any responsibility.[43] Boris Johnson has

40 Jeannette Jiang, Emily Peterson, and Robert Heimer, "COVID-19 Updated Data and Developments—March 23, 2020," Yale School of Public Health, March 23, 2020, https://ysph.yale.edu/news-article/covid-19-updated-data-and-developments---march-23-2020/.

41 Robert Cuffe, "Coronavirus Death Rate: What Are the Chances of Dying?" *BBC*, March 24, 2020, https://www.bbc.com/news/health-51674743.

42 Paul Gallagher, "Covid Inquiry: 'Professor Lockdown' Neil Ferguson Denies Urging UK-Wide Restrictions after '500k Deaths' Model," *iNews*, October 17, 2023, https://inews.co.uk/news/health/professor-lockdown-denies-uk-restrictions-model-predicted-500k-deaths-2693514.

43 Devi Sridhar, "Don't Blame Scientists for What Went Wrong with Covid—Ministers Were the Ones Calling the Shots," *The Guardian*, June 13, 2023, https://www.theguardian.com/commentisfree/2023/jun/13/covid-inquiry-ministers-scientific-advisers.

blamed the lockdown on his advisors.[44] Liz Truss admitted it would have been "better" if "we'd gone for the Swedish model."[45] The UK Covid-19 inquiry conceded that the tough lockdown failed children,[46] then, in Module 1 of its full report, openly criticized the absence of any cost-benefit analysis before implementing a lockdown that would result in a 25% drop in GDP between February and April 2020.[47] The report is even quite blunt: "Almost every area of public life across all four nations was badly affected.... Levels of mental illness, loneliness, deprivation, and exposure to violence at home surged. Children missed out on academic learning and on precious social development."[48] Moreover and crucially, the report disavowed censorship by acknowledging that "the scientific advice received by the UK government ... was not subject to sufficient external challenge ... There was no institutional guard against the risk of conventional wisdom becoming embedded in the institutions responsible for emergency preparedness and resilience."[49]

Nudging, moreover, proved in hindsight to have been "emotionally disturbing"; it used "harrowing messages and

44 Luke McGee, "Boris Johnson Has Split from His Top Scientists on Coronavirus," *CNN*, October 13, 2020, https://edition.cnn.com/2020/10/13/uk/boris-johnson-versus-scientific-advice-intl-gbr/index.html.

45 Rob Lownie, "Liz Truss: We Should Have Followed Swedish Model on Covid," *UnHerd*, September 11, 2024, https://unherd.com/newsroom/liz-truss-we-should-have-followed-swedish-model-on-covid/.

46 Amelia Hill, "Children Were Failed by Pandemic Policies, Covid Inquiry Told," *The Guardian*, October 4, 2023, https://www.theguardian.com/uk-news/2023/oct/04/children-were-failed-by-pandemic-policies-covid-inquiry-told.

47 See Toby Green, "Did the Covid Inquiry Report Just Admit Lockdown Was a Mistake?" *UnHerd*, July 18, 2024, https://unherd.com/newsroom/did-the-covid-inquiry-report-just-admit-lockdown-was-a-mistake/. The original report, Baroness Hallett, ed., *UK Covid-19 Inquiry, Module 1: The Resilience and Preparedness of the United Kingdom*, July 2024, can be found here: https://covid19.public-inquiry.uk/wp-content/uploads/2024/07/18095012/UK-Covid-19-Inquiry-Module-1-Full-Report.pdf.

48 Hallett, *UK Covid-19 Inquiry*, viii.

49 Hallett, *UK Covid-19 Inquiry*, 147.

videos ... without any ethical oversight."[50] Members of the SPI-B group mentioned in Chapter 1 who were interviewed by Laura Dodsworth expressed "regret" over their action. For instance, Gavin Morgan, a psychologist, admitted that "using fear as a means of control is not ethical. Using fear smacks of totalitarianism."[51] Another one told Laura Dodsworth that the way in which fear was "ramped up" to "encourage compliance" was "dystopian."[52] A third warned about the "authoritarianism" that was "creeping in."[53] And finally, one told her, members of SPI-B were "stunned by the weaponization of behavioral psychology" during the pandemic, and "psychologists didn't seem to notice when it stopped being altruistic and became manipulative. They have too much power, and it intoxicates them."[54] This lucid analysis speaks for itself.

In the US, former president Trump blamed the lockdown on Anthony Fauci.[55] He famously declared, "I don't take responsibility at all."[56] Andrew Cuomo, the governor of New York and beacon of the liberal left opposition to President Trump, declared having done what was possible in an atmosphere of disinformation.[57] Former NIH director Francis

50 Sidley, "UK Government Use of Behavioral Science."

51 Gordon Rayner, "Use of Fear to Control Behavior in Covid Crisis was 'Totalitarian,' Admit Scientists," *The Telegraph*, May 14, 2021, https://www.telegraph.co.uk/news/2021/05/14/scientists-admit-totalitarian-use-fear-control-behaviour-covid/. See also Dodsworth, *A State of Fear*.

52 Rayner, "Use of Fear to Control Behavior."

53 Rayner, "Use of Fear to Control Behavior."

54 Rayner, "Use of Fear to Control Behavior."

55 Kaitlan Collins and Kevin Liptak, "Trump Trashes Fauci and Makes Baseless Coronavirus Claims in Campaign Call," *CNN*, October 20, 2020, https://edition.cnn.com/2020/10/19/politics/donald-trump-anthony-fauci-coronavirus/index.html.

56 Amber Phillips, "Everyone and Everything Trump Has Blamed for His Coronavirus Response," *The Washington Post*, March 31, 2020, https://www.washingtonpost.com/politics/2020/03/31/everyone-everything-trump-has-blamed-his-coronavirus-response/.

57 Real Time with Bill Maher, "Overtime: Andrew Cuomo, Scott Galloway, Melissa

Collins admitted on the lockdown policy that "public health people had a very narrow view of what the right decision is"[58] and that "we were not really thinking about the consequences (of the lockdown) in communities that were not New York City or some other big city."[59] Anthony Fauci held on ABC News that he had "nothing to do with closing down schools."[60] The Select Subcommittee on the Coronavirus Pandemic was irritated by Dr. Fauci's "feigned ignorance," picking up on his "not recalling" events and issues around the pandemic "more than 100 times" in his congressional testimonies.[61] But he did admit in front of the same subcommittee on June 4, 2024, that he couldn't recall any scientific research supporting evidence for masking children. He also conceded that the six-foot social distancing guideline, which made it nearly impossible for schools to reopen, was "arbitrary" and "not based on science."[62] In Australia, former New South Wales Premier, Dominic Perrotet, declared upon retiring that the Covid vaccine mandate his government had enforced was "wrong."[63]

Courts are now regularly vindicating the complaints of citizens and groups who felt robbed of their rights by overly

---

DeRosa," YouTube video, 17:05, October 28, 2023, https://www.youtube.com/watch?v=QQApZhXLcic.

58 Jeff Jacoby, "A Pandemic Mea Culpa from Francis Collins," *Boston Globe*, January 21, 2024, https://www.bostonglobe.com/2024/01/21/opinion/jeff-jacoby-francis-collins-anthony-fauci-covid/.

59 Jacoby, "A Pandemic Mea Culpa."

60 The Hill, "Fauci: I Had 'Nothing to Do' with Covid School Shutdowns, Blames the Media," YouTube video, 9:17, October 17, 2022, https://www.youtube.com/watch?v=W9rsSanDrR8.

61 COVID Select Committee, "Press Release: COVID Select Subcommittee Releases Dr. Fauci's Transcript, Highlights Key Takeaways in New Memo," May 31, 2024, https://oversight.house.gov/release/covid-select-subcommittee-releases-dr-faucis-transcript-highlights-key-takeaways-in-new-memo/.

62 Select Committee, "Press Release."

63 Flat White, "Perrotet's Covid Apology Is Not Good Enough," *The Spectator Australia*, August 7, 2024, https://www.spectator.com.au/2024/08/perrottets-covid-apology-is-not-good-enough.

authoritarian measures, for instance, a Frenchman who was prevented from visiting his dying father because of the stay-at-home orders.[64] In June 2024, the *New York Times* published a piece by lockdown critic Alec MacGillis which emphasized that the lockdowns had led to mass starvation in poor countries and finally stated the key question which should have been posed from the start: "Were the public health benefits of lockdowns and quarantines worth it, considering their destructive impacts on people's ability to feed their families?"[65]

In January 2022, Anthony Fauci co-authored an article acknowledging the inefficacy of the Covid vaccine in preventing transmission and re-infection, which was quite a stunning admission.[66] A Pfizer executive, Janine Small (representing Pfizer CEO Albert Bourla, who refused to come in person), was asked in front of the EU Parliament Special Committee on the COVID-19 Pandemic if Pfizer tested the Covid vaccine for transmission of the virus before it entered the market. She testified: "Regarding the question around did we know about stopping immunization before it entered the market, no. We had to really move at the speed of science to really understand what is taking place in the market."[67]

---

64 See "Covid-19: l'État condamné pour avoir empêché un homme de voir son père mourant pendant le confinement," *Le Figaro*, February 15, 2024, https://www.lefigaro.fr/actualite-france/covid-19-l-etat-condamne-pour-avoir-empeche-un-homme-de-voir-son-pere-mourant-pendant-le-confinement-20240215.

65 Alec MacGillis, "There's Food for Everyone on Earth. So Why Is Hunger Getting Worse?" *The Washington Post*, June 24, 2024, https://www.nytimes.com/2024/06/24/books/review/the-new-breadline-jean-martin-bauer.html.

66 David M. Morens, Jeffrey K. Tautenberger, and Anthony Fauci, "Universal Coronavirus Vaccine—An Urgent Need," *New England Journal of Medicine*, January 27, 2022, https://www.nejm.org/doi/full/10.1056/NEJMp2118468.

67 See the Twitter post of MEP member Rob Roos (@Rob_Roos), "Breaking: vaccine never tested on preventing transmission. This means the COVID passport was based on a big lie," Twitter, October 11, 2022, 11:04 am, https://twitter.com/Rob_Roos/status/1579759795225198593.

Various health authorities, such as Jean-François Delfraissy, the head of the French Covid task force, later admitted that they had been aware from the outset that vaccines would not significantly reduce transmission, even though curbing transmission was a primary public health argument used to encourage vaccine uptake.[68] Paul Offit, a member of the FDA Vaccine Advisory Committee, which approved the Covid vaccine, and a former member of the CDC, one of the officials who was most involved in promoting the Covid vaccine, claimed in March 2024 that the Covid vaccine should have been recommended only for the elderly and high-risk groups, but:

> The language ... morphed to essentially a universal recommendation for everyone over six months of age ... I actually talked to Dr Fauci about this particular issue.... He said when you give a nuanced message like that, it's a garbled message. You're much more likely to be able to convince those high-risk groups to get it if you recommend it for everybody.[69]

So this is how a vaccine which was not considered necessary for a majority of the population was recommended, and sometimes made mandatory, for groups of the population that did not need it and for whom it was possibly dangerous.

Major mainstream outlets like the *New York Times* and the *Guardian* ignored Janine Small's testimony, but the *Daily Wire* called the Pfizer executive's response "scandalous."[70] On

---

68 L'invité, "Jean-François Delfraissy: 'La vérité sur le Covid, les vaccins et les tartuffes de la télé,'" YouTube video, 32:27, October 12, 2023, https://www.youtube.com/watch?app=desktop&v=6hdOAE_0BiU.

69 Doctor Mike, "The Uncomfortable Truth of What Actually Happened with COVID—Dr. Paul Offit," YouTube video, 1:53:56, March 24, 2024, https://www.youtube.com/watch?v=_OF6vP-SkGA.

70 Greg Wilson, "'Scandalous': Pfizer Exec Tells EU Lawmaker COVID Jab Was Never Tested to Show It Blocked Transmission," *The Daily Wire*, October 12, 2022, https://www.dailywire.com/news/scandalous-pfizer-exec-tells-eu-lawmaker-covid-jab-was-never-tested-to-show-it-blocked-transmission.

the other hand, reports suggesting that Pfizer had not tested the vaccine for transmission were dismissed as "fake news" by Associated Press and Reuters, despite a wide sharing of Janine Small's interview clips on social media.[71] Meanwhile, another viral clip circulating on social media compiled headlines from around the world, ridiculing the diminishing efficacy claims of the vaccine. These headlines showcased a rapid decline in promised efficacy rates, plummeting from an initial 95% promise down to 20% within a few months. This decline in efficacy formed an inversely proportional curve compared to Pfizer's soaring profits, however, which reached new heights.[72]

In the Czech Republic, the Constitutional Court judged illegal the banning of a father from the birth of his child and ruled that "the father's participation in the birth is part of the right to family life."[73] The President of the Constitutional Court Josef Baxa deemed the Covid measures exaggerated to the point of "recalling the time of non-freedom," a common Czech euphemism for the communist regime.[74]

---

71 Melissa Goldin and Angelo Fichera, "Posts Mislead on Pfizer COVID Vaccine's Impact on Transmission," AP Fact Check, October 14, 2024, https://apnews.com/article/fact-check-pfizer-transmission-european-parliament-950413863226; Reuters Fact Check, "Fact Check: Preventing Transmission Never Required for COVID Vaccines' Initial Approval; Pfizer Vax Did Reduce Transmission of Early Variants," February 12, 2024, https://www.reuters.com/fact-check/preventing-transmission-never-required-covid-vaccines-initial-approval-pfizer-2024-02-12/.

72 See the Twitter post of Prashant Bhushan (@pbhushan1), "Watch: Vaccine efficacy in 2 minutes!" Twitter, October 23, 2021, 9:06 am, https://twitter.com/pbhushan1/status/1451807240659161090?lang=en.

73 (čtk), "ÚS o zákazu při epidemii covidu: Otec má právo být u porodu," *Česká justice*, May 31, 2023, https://www.ceska-justice.cz/2023/05/us-o-zakazu-pri-epidemii-covidu-otec-ma-pravo-byt-u-porodu/.

74 (čtk), "Mimořádná opatření podle Baxy s nadsázkou dávají vzpomenout na dobu nesvobody," *Česká justice*, July 1, 2021, https://www.ceska-justice.cz/2021/07/mimoradna-opatreni-podle-baxy-s-nadsazkou-davaji-vzpomenout-na-dobu-nesvobody/.

The unreflective role of the liberal press: Virtue-signaling in place of investigation

While some members of SPI-B demonstrate reflexivity and self-criticism, this sentiment is not universal, particularly among the mainstream press. The *Atlantic* pleaded for "a pandemic amnesty" because "we just didn't know,"[75] which is rather brazen considering the condescending and sometimes venomous headlines the paper had published for years.

Liberal mainstream media weaponized Covid victims for political purposes. The *New York Times* had exhibited so little interest in the first 100,000 deaths from AIDS in 1991 that it had run only a short item on page 18.[76] The first 1,000 victims of Covid, on the other hand, were spread out one by one across the entire front page of the *New York Times* with the caption "U.S. Deaths Near 100,000, An Incalculable Loss," calling it a "grim milestone," which mainly served to underscore the incompetence of the Trump administration.[77]

Scott Galloway, a New York University professor who had been a passionate advocate of lockdowns and masks, claimed on Real Time with Bill Maher (HBO) on October 27, 2023:

> We were all operating with imperfect information, and we were doing our best. Let's learn from it, let's hold each other accountable, but let's bring a little bit of grace and forgiveness to the shitshow that was Covid.[78]

---

75 Emily Oster, "Let's Declare a Pandemic Amnesty," *The Atlantic*, October 20, 2022, https://www.theatlantic.com/ideas/archive/2022/10/covid-response-forgiveness/671879/.

76 AP, "U.S. Reports AIDS Deaths Now Exceed 100,000," *The New York Times*, January 25, 1991, https://www.nytimes.com/1991/01/25/us/us-reports-aids-deaths-now-exceed-100000.html.

77 "An Incalculable Loss," *The New York Times*, May 27, 2020, https://www.nytimes.com/interactive/2020/05/24/us/us-coronavirus-deaths-100000.html.

78 "Overtime: Andrew Cuomo, Scott Galloway, Melissa DeRosa. Real Time with Bill Maher (HBO)," October 28, 2023, https://www.youtube.com/watch?v=Q-QApZhXLcic.

A claim to imperfection is legitimate, but it is troubling that no cost-benefit analysis of the measure was ever performed by authorities in the countries that advocated the lockdown most stridently.[79] Scott Galloway operated with "imperfect information" for the good reason that his favorite outlets suppressed any criticism of the Covid official policy and derided them as "fake news," while calling for ever more censorship.[80]

Uri Berliner, a journalist at National Public Radio for 25 years, described how virtue-signaling came to take the place of investigative journalism at NPR so that the latter now defaults to "ideological story lines."[81] One of the three examples he takes concerns the lab leak theory of the coronavirus in Wuhan, China, opposing "Team Natural Origin" to "Team Lab Leak." He describes how the lab leak theory was instantly dismissed as "racist or a right-wing conspiracy theory": it was enough that Francis Collins and Anthony Fauci, who represented the medical establishment, had spoken against it for NPR to endorse their point of view.[82] NPR also refrained from mentioning that many of the scientists it interviewed reported doubts about the natural origin story in private or that the Energy Department concluded, even if with low confidence, that the lab leak was the most probable explanation: "Instead, we introduced our coverage of that development on February 28, 2023, by asserting confidently that 'the scientific evidence overwhelmingly points to a natural origin for the virus.'"[83]

---

79 *The Spectator*, "Covid and the Politics of Panic."

80 See Lisa O'Carroll, "EU Warns Elon Musk after Twitter Found to Have Highest Rate of Disinformation," *The Guardian*, September 26, 2023, https://www.theguardian.com/technology/2023/sep/26/eu-warns-elon-musk-that-twitter-x-must-comply-with-fake-news-laws.

81 Uri Berliner, "I've Been at NPR for 25 Years. Here's How We Lost America's Trust," *The Free Press*, April 17, 2024, https://www.thefp.com/p/npr-editor-how-npr-lost-americas-trust.

82 Berliner, "I've Been at NPR for 25 Years."

83 Berliner, "I've Been at NPR for 25 Years." See also, for instance, Geoff Brumfiel,

In short, "advocacy groups are given a seat at the table in determining the terms and vocabulary of our news coverage."[84] Uri Berliner was so criticized as a result of his critical piece that he resigned from NPR a few days later.[85]

Marianne Klowak, a veteran reporter from the Canadian Broadcasting Corporation, testified during the Canadian National Citizens Inquiry that she felt journalists had betrayed the public and broken their trust by branding the doctors and the experts the CBC chose as "competent and trustworthy," while those who challenged the narrative were presented as dangerous and spreading disinformation. Her conclusion is without appeal: "I felt like I had failed these people, as a journalist, to give voice to their truth, so I witnessed in a very short time the collapse of journalism.... The way I saw it, we were in fact pushing propaganda."[86]

As noted above, the Israeli liberal newspaper *Haaretz* offers insightful reflections on the role of the media within censorious and authoritarian contexts. Mindful of the challenge of dissenting from national consensus and the latter's associated privileges, *Haaretz* underscored how critics face scrutiny on social media.[87] It criticized other Israeli media outlets for functioning as a "kind of national public relations division," overly focused on propagating the government's narrative rather than fulfilling their vital democratic role of identifying

---

"Scientists Debunk Lab Accident Theory of Pandemic Emergence," *NPR*, April 22, 2020, https://www.npr.org/2020/04/22/841925672/scientists-debunk-lab-accident-theory-of-pandemic-emergence.

84 Berliner, "I've Been at NPR for 25 Years."

85 Benjamin Mullin and Katie Robertson, "NPR in Turmoil after It Is Accused of Liberal Bias," *The Washington Post*, April 11, 2024, https://www.nytimes.com/2024/04/11/business/media/npr-criticism-liberal-bias.html.

86 TheOriginalMxGForce, "Former CBC Reporter Marianne Klowak Admits That the Media Manipulated Citizens during COVID," YouTube video, 2:35, August 29, 2024, https://www.youtube.com/watch?v=ifmqdOR1-JU.

87 Ring, "The Militarization of the Coronavirus Crisis."

failures, preventing abuses of power during crises, and advocating for the marginalized.[88] The conclusion of journalist Edan Ring is that the "media's self-censorship, its turning a blind eye to the blow to basic civil rights and the rule of law" posed a "genuine danger to all citizens."[89] While the media focused on reporting case numbers and ventilators, Shin Bet implemented intrusive surveillance measures.[90]

At which point does media silence amount to being complicit?

The *New York Times* contends that resisting censorship enforced by social media platforms under the direction of the American government to suppress criticism of its Covid policies constitutes "disinformation." It suggests that freedom of speech, protected by the First Amendment, is now an "unsettled question."[91] If opposing censorship becomes akin to spreading disinformation, we might indeed seriously question the purpose of the First Amendment. Traditional media appear more interested in restoring their de facto monopoly on political commentary in the public sphere by silencing social media than in defending free speech as a principle. In the case at hand, it is the *New York Times* itself which has been spreading disinformation: Mark Zuckerberg, the Facebook CEO, was pressed by the House Committee on the Judiciary, which is investigating this censorship on social media at the behest of the US government (see Chapter 2). As briefly mentioned above, in August 2024 he wrote in a letter to Jim Jordan, chair of this committee, in which he confirmed the results of the committee inquiry:

---

88 Ring, "The Militarization of the Coronavirus Crisis."

89 Ring, "The Militarization of the Coronavirus Crisis."

90 Ring, "The Militarization of the Coronavirus Crisis."

91 Jim Rutenberg and Steven Lee Myers, "How Trump's Allies Are Winning the War over Disinformation," *The Washington Post*, March 17, 2024, https://www.nytimes.com/2024/03/17/us/politics/trump-disinformation-2024-social-media.html.

> In 2021, senior officials from the Biden Administration, including the White House, repeatedly pressured our teams for months to censor certain Covid-19 contents, including humor and satire, and expressed a lot of frustration with our teams when we didn't agree.... I believe the government pressure was wrong, and I regret that we were not more outspoken about it. I also think we made some choices that, with the benefit of hindsight and new information, we wouldn't make today.[92]

In Europe, EU Internal Market Commissioner Thierry Breton sent a letter to Elon Musk when the latter held an interview with presidential candidate Donald Trump on Twitter on August 13, 2024. In the context of "potential risks in the EU associated with the dissemination of content that may incite violence, hate, and racism," he summoned Musk to "promptly ensure the effectiveness of your systems" concerning "content moderation" or face even stricter "ongoing proceedings" of the EU against Twitter.[93] Breton immediately faced accusations of meddling in the US election and was slapped down by European Commission president Ursula von der Leyen for not seeking her approval before sending the letter.[94] He actually resigned a few days later, but he clearly appears to favor more censorship in the future.

In yet another example of governmental meddling into free speech issues, Telegram founder and CEO Pavel Durov

92 See the Twitter post of the House Judiciary GOP group which reproduced the letter in full, House Judiciary GOP (@JudiciaryGOP), "Mark Zuckerberg just admitted three things," Twitter, August 27, 2024, 12:44 am, https://x.com/JudiciaryGOP/status/1828201780544504064.

93 The letter was paradoxically published by Thierry Breton on his Twitter account, Thierry Breton (@ThierryBreton), "With great audience comes greater responsibility #DSA," August 12, 2024, 6:25 pm, https://x.com/ThierryBreton/status/1823033048109367549.

94 Alice Hancock, "Brussels Slaps Down Thierry Breton over 'Harmful Content' Letter to Elon Musk, *Financial Times*, August 13, 2024, https://www.ft.com/content/09cf4713-7199-4e47-a373-ed5de61c2afa.

was arrested in Paris in August 2024 and charged for failing to censor child pornography on Telegram[95]—an ironic contradiction of the fact that Durov had been granted French citizenship in 2021 in recognition of his resistance to the censorship demands of the Putin regime, which had prompted his departure into exile.

Another startling element is the complacency of mainstream liberal media regarding the investigation of the financial interests involved in the pharmaceutical industry's capture of public health, particularly concerning the Covid vaccine. I interpret this passivity at least partly as a detrimental consequence of censorship on Covid policies. Influential outlets like the *New York Times*, the *Guardian*, and the *Washington Post* have been confined by the official narrative they have endorsed. By acquiescing in the censorship of dissenting voices associated with "Trump supporters," a stance influenced by disdain for these voters (exemplified by Hillary Clinton's characterization of this segment of the public as "the deplorables"), these media outlets have hindered their own ability to provide a critical perspective. Unlike during the Watergate scandal, when it was the *Washington Post*'s relentless investigation which exposed Nixon, mainstream media's adherence to political and ideological dogmas now undermines their journalistic integrity. Instead, genuinely investigative journalists like Glenn Greenwald, Paul D. Thacker, Alex Berenson, Matt Taibbi, and others are now thriving on Substack or other channels.

95 France 24 and AFP, "Arrestation de Pavel Durov: Emmanuel Macron nie toute 'décision politique,'" August 26, 2024, *France24.com*, https://www.france24.com/fr/europe/20240826-arrestation-de-pavel-durov-emmanuel-macron-nie-toute-d%C3%A9cision-politique.

The lab leak theory deserves to be thoroughly investigated

Despite the best efforts of the liberal press, the lab leak theory is now gaining track. Inquiries as to the origins of the Covid virus repeatedly bring to light that the US National Institutes of Health funded research on viruses in China, possibly even on bioweapons. How did this come about?

After a bird flu outbreak in 2011, Anthony Fauci, director of the NIAID, Francis Collins, director of NIH, and Gary J. Nabel, director of the Vaccine Research Center at NIAID, co-authored an article in the *Washington Post*, praising lab research on the bird flu virus and its potential transmission to humans and supporting the notion that generating a "potentially dangerous virus in the laboratory" would bring "important information and insights." It was, they wrote, a "risk worth taking." [96]

But in 2014, the Obama administration instituted a moratorium on research on these dangerous viruses, which "came in the wake of some high-profile lab mishaps at the Centers for Disease Control and Prevention, plus some extremely controversial flu experiments."[97] NPR interviewed a scientist specialist of the coronaviruses SARS and MERS, Ralph Baric. He was shocked, as eighteen grants of the NIH were suddenly banned. But another microbiologist, David Relman, claimed that the government was "right to include SARS and MERS in this moratorium, because they are so close to being

---

96 Anthony S. Fauci, Gary J. Nabel, and Francis S. Collins, "A Flu Virus Risk Worth Taking," *The Washington Post*, December 30, 2011, https://www.washingtonpost.com/opinions/a-flu-virus-risk-worth-taking/2011/12/30/gIQAM9sNRP_story.html.

97 Nell Greenfieldboyce, "How a Tilt Toward Safety Stopped a Scientist's Virus Research," *NPR*, November 7, 2014, https://www.npr.org/sections/health-shots/2014/11/07/361219361/how-a-tilt-toward-safety-stopped-a-scientists-virus-research.

pandemic viruses." Only one "trait" was missing: "their means of transmitting easily between humans."[98]

In 2021, the *Intercept* obtained documents showing that the Wuhan Institute of Virology was engaged in "gain of function" research on viruses thanks to grant money from the NIH, specifically from the NIAID headed by Anthony Fauci, via EcoHealth Alliance, a "research organization which studies the spread of viruses from animals to humans."[99]

China is not known as the US's most friendly ally, but, as Anthony Fauci put it with surprising candor, "You don't want to go to Hoboken, New Jersey or to Fairfax, Virginia to be studying the bat-human interface that might lead to an outbreak, so you go to China."[100] The Chinese regime didn't seem to mind. Even the US Department of Health and Human Services, albeit only in 2023, appears to have recognized the imprudence of funding the Wuhan Institute of Health in these conditions and reversed its decision.[101] Regardless of whether the virus originated from the Wuhan lab,[102] the act of displacing the risk onto a population without their consultation was ethically dubious in the first place.

98 Greenfieldboyce, "A Tilt Toward Safety."

99 Sharon Lerner, Mara Hvistendahl, and Maia Hibbett, "NIH Documents Provide New Evidence U.S. Funded Gain-of-Function Research in Wuhan," *The Intercept*, September 9, 2021, https://theintercept.com/2021/09/09/covid-origins-gain-of-function-research.

100 Leland Vittert and Mike Ewing, "Dr. Anthony Fauci Responds to Criticism of Wuhan Lab Funding, Release of Thousands of His Emails," *The Donlon Report*, June 2, 2021, https://www.newsnationnow.com/the-donlon-report/dr-anthony-fauci-responds-to-criticism-of-wuhan-lab-funding-release-of-thousands-of-his-emails/ (the full interview with Dr Fauci is accessible on this page.)

101 Sarah Knapton, "China Lab Suspected of Covid Leak Stripped of US Funding for Violating Biosafety Rules," *The Telegraph*, September 24, 2023, https://www.telegraph.co.uk/world-news/2023/09/24/china-lab-wuhan-leaking-covid-loses-us-funding-experiments/.

102 Jeremy Herb and Natasha Bertrand, "US Energy Department Assesses Covid-19 Likely Resulted from Lab Leak, Furthering US Intel Divide over Virus Origin," *CNN*, February 27, 2023, https://edition.cnn.com/2023/02/26/politics/covid-lab-leak-wuhan-china-intelligence/index.html.

The House of Representatives' Select Subcommittee on the Coronavirus Pandemic conducted two interviews with Peter Daszak regarding a potential lab leak at the Wuhan Institute of Virology at the time when the Covid outbreak began. Daszak, head of the biotech firm EcoHealth Alliance mentioned above, was the one who hired and oversaw researchers in Wuhan who were studying bat viruses with this funding from the National Institutes of Health. The reasons behind American agencies funding a Chinese lab, the nature of the research conducted there, which could include bioweapons, the involvement of Anthony Fauci in this funding, and his knowledge of the research are critical questions. Yet, the mainstream press has largely neglected to investigate these issues, bringing us yet again back to Chimamanda Ngozi Adichie's "end of curiosity." The implication that Americans might have played a role in the Covid outbreak, if only by incompetence or negligence, is nevertheless momentous, so Congress's interest is keen.

The Select Subcommittee published an interim report in which it stated: "The below report provides extensive evidence ... that EcoHealth's actions were often enabled by the incompetency of the National Institutes of Health and the National Institute of Allergy and Infectious Diseases. It is this contempt and incompetence that necessitates both congressional and administrative action."[103]

During his second hearing in May 2024, Peter Daszak faced relentless questioning, and several inconsistencies emerged compared to his testimony six months earlier. This time, both Republicans and Democrats scrutinized him

103 Select Subcommittee on the Coronavirus Pandemic Committee on Oversight and Accountability, "An Evaluation of the Evidence Surrounding EcoHealth Alliance, Inc.'s Research Activities," May 1, 2024, https://oversight.house.gov/wp-content/uploads/2024/04/2024.05.01-SSCP-Report_FINAL.pdf.

rigorously. Following this interview, the Select Subcommittee concluded in its report:

> Dr. Daszak repeatedly violated the terms of the NIH grant awarded to EcoHealth. The report recommended the formal debarment of and a criminal investigation into EcoHealth and Dr. Daszak. During the hearing, members questioned Dr. Daszak about the findings of this report, pressed him to explain EcoHealth's relationship with the Wuhan Institute of Virology, and scrutinized his abuse of U.S. taxpayer dollars to fund dangerous, potentially pandemic-causing research. Staff from both the majority and the minority grilled Daszak on his less than forthcoming testimony to Congress and described evidence showing EcoHealth "absolutely" facilitated "gain-of-function" research at the WIV on the American taxpayer's dime.[104]

It is unclear as of September 2024 if the investigation of the lab leak theory will be fully solved one way or the other, but the mainstream media's enduring apathy toward this possibility is remarkable. It is as though the narrative of the zoonotic origin promoted by Anthony Fauci in March 2020 was beyond reproach,[105] despite Fauci's acknowledgment during his own January 2024 testimony before the same Subcommittee that the lab leak theory is not a conspiracy theory but a plausible scenario.[106] Jay Bhattacharya, one of the Great Barrington Declaration authors, reconstructed the Covid outbreak as if

---

104 Select Subcommittee on the Coronavirus Pandemic, "Heading Wrap Up: EcoHealth Alliance Should be Criminally Investigated, Formally Debarred," May 3, 2024, https://oversight.house.gov/release/hearing-wrap-up-ecohealth-alliance-should-be-criminally-investigated-formally-debarred/.

105 See Kristian G. Andersen et. al, "The Proximal Origin of SARS-CoV-2," *Nature Medicine* 26, no. 450-452 (2020), https://www.nature.com/articles/s41591-020-0820-9.

106 See the Twitter post of the Select Subcommittee, Select Subcommittee on the Coronavirus Pandemic (COVIDSelect), "Dr. Fauci acknowledged that the lab-leak hypothesis is not a conspiracy theory," Twitter, January 10, 2024, 12:41 pm, https://twitter.com/COVIDSelect/status/1745048325252891068.

it had come from a lab leak—and while no one has any certainty yet, the scenario is perfectly plausible.[107] Now even the *New York Times*[108] and CNN anchor Chris Cuomo[109] (brother of Andrew Cuomo, the much publicized Democratic governor of New York during the first wave of Covid in spring 2020) seriously entertain the question, as should have been the case from the start.

It is praiseworthy for the *New York Times*, Chris Cuomo, and mainstream media in general to do so now. But it is historically quite unfair, as almost always in such circumstances, that those who did ask these questions at a time when they were critical, be it on the lab leak or, for that matter, on Covid vaccine injuries, or on ivermectin as a drug to treat Covid, were hailed as conspiracists and marginalized. While the sidelined individuals rarely regain their former careers and are often swiftly forgotten, these questions are later appropriated by the same people who marginalized them, and they are the ones who are eventually praised for their critical attitude. Truth-seekers rarely get credit. As French intellectuals know, it is "better to be wrong with Jean-Paul Sartre" (who supported Stalinist show trials but was a moral figure for revolutionary Parisian students in 1968) "than to be right with Raymond Aron" (whose analysis of communist regimes was right from the start but who never experienced quite the same fame as Jean-Paul Sartre). In other words, it pays to be an opportunist.

---

107 Jan Jekielek and Dr. Jay Bhattacharya, "Scientists Opened Pandora's Box—Now What?" *Epoch TV*, May 30, 2024, https://www.theepochtimes.com/epochtv/scientists-opened-pandoras-box-what-now-dr-jay-bhattacharya-5659468.

108 Alina Chan, "Why the Pandemic Probably Started in a Lab, in 5 Key Points," *The Washington Post*, June 3, 2024, https://www.nytimes.com/interactive/2024/06/03/opinion/covid-lab-leak.html.

109 See The Chris Cuomo Project, "Ex-CDC Chief Dr. Robert Redfield Reveals COVID-19 Truths," YouTube video, 1:08:46, June 5, 2024, https://www.youtube.com/watch?v=oMlhvnMpRU0.

Legal challenges to Covid measures

Covid has transcended mere virology; it has emerged as a litmus test for the resilience of our democracies, particularly in upholding scientific discourse. Four years after the beginning of the pandemic, initial legal outcomes in the United States suggest that not only social media platforms but also governmental bodies have exceeded their legal authority. Journalist and author Alex Berenson took Twitter to court for violating his First Amendment right to free speech, following his indefinite ban for alleged "disinformation."[110] Upon a federal judge's decision to allow the lawsuit to proceed, rejecting Twitter's motion to dismiss,[111] the social media giant opted to settle, reinstating Berenson's account.[112] As part of the settlement, Berenson gained access to internal Twitter documents, dubbed the "Twitter Files," which revealed that the platform censored his content at the behest of the Biden administration[113]—a revelation scarcely covered, if at all, by the mainstream press.

In the case of Missouri vs. Biden, filed in 2022 and later renamed Murthy vs. Missouri,[114] the argument for defending free

110 See "Alex Berenson v. Twitter, Inc," *Digital Commons*, December 20, 2021, https://digitalcommons.law.scu.edu/cgi/viewcontent.cgi?article=3601&context=historical.

111 Judge Alsup, "Order Re: 27 Motion to Dismiss," *GovInfo*, April 29, 2022, https://www.govinfo.gov/app/details/USCOURTS-cand-3_21-cv-09818/context.

112 Kaitlyn Tiffany, "A Prominent Vaccine Sceptic Returns to Twitter," *The Atlantic*, August 24, 2022, https://www.theatlantic.com/technology/archive/2022/08/alex-berenson-twitter-ban-lawsuit-covid-misinformation671219/.

113 Melissa Koenig, "Twitter Files Dump Shows Company SUPPRESSED Debate and Information from Doctors and Experts Which Clashed with White House—and Suspended Vaccine Skeptic Alex Berenson at Biden's Request," *The Daily Mail*, December 26, 2022, https://www.dailymail.co.uk/news/article-11574573/Twitter-suppressed-covid-information-doctors-experts.html.

114 "State of Missouri et. al versus Joseph R. Biden Jr., et al.," Case No. 3:22-CV-01213, July 4, 2023, https://ago.mo.gov/wp-content/uploads/missouri-v-biden-ruling.pdf. See also Clay Calvert, "Missouri v. Biden and the Crossroads of Politics, Censorship and Free Speech," *The Hill*, September 13, 2023, https://

speech as guaranteed by the First Amendment centered on allegations of censorship against critics of Covid policies by the US government via the conduit of social media platforms. In other words, the plaintiffs charged that the White House collaborated with social media giants to suppress free speech. Judge Terry A. Doughty of the Fifth Circuit issued a preliminary injunction against the Biden administration on July 4, 2023, limiting administration officials from communicating with social media. This decision was justified on the grounds that:

> The Plaintiffs are likely to succeed on the merits in establishing that the Government has used its power to silence the opposition. Opposition to Covid-19 vaccines; opposition to Covid-19 masking and lockdowns; opposition to the lab-leak theory of Covid-19.... All were suppressed. It is quite telling that each example or category of suppressed speech was conservative in nature. This targeted suppression of conservative ideas is a perfect example of viewpoint discrimination of political speech. American citizens have the right to engage in free debate about the significant issues affecting the country. If the allegations made by plaintiffs are true, the present case arguably involves the most massive attack against free speech in United States' history.[115]

The injunction initially blocked the US government from communicating with social media companies, prompting the Department of Justice to file an appeal seeking a stay. In September 2023, the Fifth Circuit upheld the district court ruling against the Biden administration on appeal but narrowed

---

thehill.com/opinion/judiciary/4198285-missouri-v-biden-and-the-crossroads-of-politics-censorship-and-free-speech/.

115 See Judge Terry A. Doughty, "State of Missouri et. al. vs. Joseph R. Biden et. al.: Judgment," United States District Court, Western Division of Louisiana, Monroe Division, July 4, 2023, https://int.nyt.com/data/documenttools/injunction-in-missouri-et-al-v/7ba314723d052bc4/full.pdf.

down the injunction, deeming it overly broad.[116] After the Department of Justice appealed again, the Supreme Court agreed in October 2023 to hear the case, while simultaneously lifting the injunction. Oral arguments from both parties were heard in March 2024 in a strained atmosphere.[117] On the eve of this hearing, the *New York Times* showcased its virtuous horror, suggesting that only "friends of Mr. Trump" would criticize Biden's Covid policy. It further asserted, as mentioned above, that the First Amendment guaranteeing the right to free speech was an "unsettled question."[118]

Given the intensity of the debate, the Supreme Court was divided on the issue. The judgment regarding this injunction (only the injunction) was handed on June 26, 2024, with six justices against three. It ruled that the plaintiffs had no standing in their request to prevent the Biden administration from contacting social media, as they could not prove a "direct injury."[119] In other words, the Supreme Court defined a new threshold for standing (i.e., for having a justified motivation to sue), one in which the government is allowed to demand censorship of particular ideas from social media as long as it doesn't target a particular person by name.[120]

---

116 Tiemey Sneed, "Appeals Court Says Biden Admin Likely Violated First Amendment but Narrows Order Blocking Officials from Communicating with Social Media Companies," *CNN*, September 9, 2023, https://edition.cnn.com/2023/09/08/politics/biden-administration-social-media-lawsuit/index.html.

117 See the analysis of the case by two of the plaintiffs, Aaron Kheriaty and Jay Bhattacharya, on *The Illusion of Consensus* podcast, "Aaron Kheriaty on the Murthy vs. Missouri Supreme Court Hearing," April 2, 2024, https://www.illusionconsensus.com/p/episode-43-aaron-kheriaty-on-the.

118 Rutenberg and Myers, "How Trump's Allies Are Winning." See also the Wikipedia page "Murthy v. Missouri," https://en.wikipedia.org/wiki/Murthy_v._Missouri#:~:text=On%20July%204%2C%202023%2C%20Judge,for%20material%20involving%20illegal%20activity.

119 Supreme Court of the United States, "Murthy, Surgeon General, et al. v. Missouri et al. Certiorari to the United States Court of Appeals for the Fifth Circuit," June 26, 2024, https://www.supremecourt.gov/opinions/23pdf/23-411_3dq3.pdf.

120 See Aaron Kheriaty's second podcast with Jay Bhattacharya, "The Worst

The injunction was therefore lifted, and the Biden administration was allowed anew to contact social media in order to "combat misinformation," which the *New York Times* hailed as a "major practical victory" for President Biden,[121] while the original trial of Murthy vs. Missouri resumed. A new element, however, was that Robert F. Kennedy Jr., who was also suing the federal government for restriction of his own free speech as a presidential candidate, asked to have his lawsuit Kennedy vs. Biden consolidated with the Murthy vs. Missouri case (actually against Jay Bhattacharya and Aaron Kheriaty's will, who feared politicization of their case), so he effectively became their co-plaintiff.

A positive element for the Missouri side is that Kennedy immediately convinced the court that he had standing to sue the federal government, and it is enough if one of the plaintiffs has standing to grant standing to the whole case, so Missouri now also has standing. As a result, Kennedy was granted a new preliminary injunction by Judge Doughty in August 2024 to restrain contacts between the federal government and social media: "The Court finds that Kennedy is likely to succeed on his claim that suppression of content posted was caused by actions of Government Defendants, and there is a substantial risk that he will suffer similar injury in the near future."[122]

Violation of Free Speech Rights in US History," *The Illusion of Consensus* (podcast), August 6, 2024, https://www.illusionconsensus.com/p/new-the-worst-violation-of-free-speech.

121 Adam Liptak, "Supreme Court Rejects Challenge to Biden Administration's Contacts with Social Media Companies," *The New York Times*, June 26, 2024, https://www.nytimes.com/2024/06/26/us/politics/supreme-court-biden-free-speech.html.

122 Joseph Mackinnon, "Court gives RFK Jr. Green Light to Sue Biden-Harris Admin over Censorship," *The Blaze*, August 23, 2024, https://www.theblaze.com/news/court-gives-rfk-jr-green-light-to-sue-biden-harris-admin-over-censorship.

If the federal government appeals and if the Supreme Court agrees to hear the case a second time, it might finally rule on the merits of the case and really answer the question: can the federal government exert censorship on individuals via social media?[123]

We can note that the three dissenting SCOTUS justices in the Murthy vs. Missouri case are also the three most conservative (Samuel Alito Jr., Clarence Thomas, and Neil Gorsuch). Does this mean that the defense of free speech is now less of a liberal concern than a conservative one? This could be part of a tectonic shift in Western politics which sees the liberal left turning toward a more authoritarian form of governmentality while the conservative right is increasingly representing not only freedom of speech but also the vote of the poor and lower middle class—as seen with Trump's electorate. I will come back to this discussion in the conclusion.

Meanwhile, Alex Berenson, once derided by the *Atlantic* as "the pandemic's wrongest man,"[124] is also suing President Biden as a continuation of his trial against Twitter.[125] The New Civil Liberties Alliance, representing media outlets like the *Daily Wire* and the *Federalist*, along with the state of Texas, has also taken legal action against the State Department for violating free speech and press rights. Despite facing opposition, including a motion to dismiss and a request to transfer the trial venue, the Alliance prevailed on May 7, 2024, securing expedited discovery and ensuring the lawsuit will proceed.[126]

---

123 See Hannes Sarv, "Dr. Aaron Kheriaty. Censorship, Covid Crisis and the Decline of Liberal Democracies," *Freedom Research* (podcast), September 3, 2024, https://www.freedom-research.org/p/freedom-research-podcast-14-dr-aaron.

124 Derek Thompson, "The Pandemic's Wrongest Man," *The Atlantic*, April 1, 2021, https://www.theatlantic.com/ideas/archive/2021/04/pandemics-wrongest-man/618475/.

125 "Berenson v. Biden, Jr. et al.," *Justia*, April 12, 2023, https://dockets.justia.com/docket/new-york/nysdce/1:2023cv03048/597054.

126 "NCLA Defeats Motion to Dismiss, Wins Expedited Discovery in Suit Alleging

Finally, on June 18, 2024, it was announced that five states, led by Kansas, were suing Pfizer for "misleading and deceptive statements" on the properties of its Covid vaccine, Comirnaty, leading people to get vaccinated without proper information and "under duress." The evidence for this accusation comes from material obtained via the Freedom of Information Act. Five main points are mentioned in the accusation:

- "Pfizer did not provide the truth":
- the vaccine was mentioned as safe for pregnant women while "in the abandoned trial of pregnant women, more than half reported a serious adverse event and more than 10% a miscarriage";
- Pfizer denied the cardio-inflammations provoked by the vaccine;
- the would-be protective effect against variants was in fact lower than 50%;
- and Pfizer claimed the vaccine "stopped transmission."[127]

Carl Heneghan, a professor of evidence-based medicine at Oxford, summarized the charges in a post on his Substack channel. Among the many points of contention concerning the clinical trials, point 14 ("Pfizer tested the booster shot on

---

State Dept. Censorship," *New Civil Liberties Alliance*, May 7, 2024, https://nclalegal.org/2024/05/ncla-defeats-motion-to-dismiss-wins-expedited-discovery-in-suit-alleging-state-dept-censorship/.

127 See Carl Heneghan and Tom Jefferson, "Five U.S. States Sue Pfizer over False Claims of Vaccine Safety and Efficacy," *The Daily Sceptic*, June 23, 2024, https://dailysceptic.org/2024/06/23/five-u-s-states-sue-pfizer-over-false-claims-of-vaccine-safety-and-efficacy/. Reuters also reported the news, albeit in a skeptical tone: Brendan Pierson, "Kansas Accuses Pfizer of Misleading Public about Covid Vaccine in Lawsuit," *Reuters*, June 17, 2024, https://www.reuters.com/legal/kansas-accuses-pfizer-misleading-public-about-covid-vaccine-lawsuit-2024-06-17/.

only 12 trial participants (out of 40,000) who were in the 65 to 85 year-old age range") and point 15 ("Pfizer did not test the booster on any participant older than 85 years old") stand out sharply.[128]

These legal challenges to the Biden administration's official narrative underscore the importance of allowing a scientific debate. They indicate at minimum that censorship was misplaced and that a debate was worth having, regardless of the scientific validity of the narratives involved. But communist history also teaches us that the rule of law is not intangible, and it can be bent in almost any direction. When the communists took over in Czechoslovakia in 1948, they had to contend with a democratic legal system. To make it conform to the new dictatorship from one day to the next, they claimed that judges had to remedy the old, now "faulty" law by applying a "teleological interpretation of the law," i.e., by taking into account the new communist values and "directing the purpose of the law towards the upcoming victory of the working class," at least until the new communist laws were passed.[129] This is an ominous example; the Supreme Court ruling on the injunction in the case Murthy vs. Missouri can similarly be interpreted as injecting "new values" (noble censorship for the good of society) into an old law (the First Amendment).

---

128 Carl Heneghan, "Kansas Attorney General Report," *Trust the Evidence* (blog), June 27, 2024, https://trusttheevidence.substack.com/p/kansas-attorney-general-report.

129 See Michal Bobek, "Conclusions: Of Form and Substance in Central European Judicial Transitions," in *Central European Judges under the European Influence: The Transformative Power of the EU Revisited*, ed. Michal Bobek (Oxford: Hart, 2015), 403.

Summary of Chapter 4

The imperative for a thorough examination of Covid measures became apparent in Chapter 4, in light of the authoritarian inclinations and erosion of democratic norms witnessed throughout the pandemic. Governments worldwide seized upon the crisis to expand their control and stifle dissent, prompting a troubling surge in repressive speech laws in Western democracies under the pretext of combating misinformation. Legal battles in the US against the White House, revealing collusion with social media platforms to suppress free speech, serve as stark reminders of the pivotal juncture at which Western societies currently stand. Now is the time to decide whether we want to safeguard democratic ideals against political encroachment.

Conclusion

Disquieting Echoes of History, or Covid and the Liberal Left

> What was frightening about the [Stalinist show trials in Moscow] was not the fact that they happened—for obviously such things are necessary in a totalitarian society—but the eagerness of Western intellectuals to justify them.
>
> George Orwell, Review of Arthur Koestler's *Darkness at Noon*

> The most radical revolutionary will become a conservative the day after the revolution.
>
> Hannah Arendt, *The New Yorker*

This volume has recounted the collateral damage of the Covid lockdowns and the neglect of vulnerable populations. It has raised concerns about potential conflicts of interest at the intersection of science, public health, and industry interests. And it has provided a short reflection on "digital authoritarianism" with an analysis of social compliance and the instrumentalization of fear, while drawing parallels to past authoritarian regimes. It has highlighted the role of censorship in maintaining control over our contemporary societies. The Covid response has revealed the ease with which authoritarian measures have been adopted by democracies, fueled by nudging and the instrumentalization of fear. Thus I underscore the urgent need for a thorough examination of Covid measures in the face of authoritarian tendencies and the erosion of democratic norms, as exemplified by legal battles against the American administration's inclination to suppress free speech. By holding on to my method of socioreflexive cultural engagement, I have tried to navigate a central line and dodge two types of conspiracy theories that divide our contemporary societies: the one from the top down, which calls nearly all criticism "disinformation," and the one from the bottom up, which calls nearly all official policies "lies."

For a historian of European authoritarian regimes, there is a sense of déjà vu in all this. The repressive and censoring measures which multiplied under the pretext of Covid but took a life of their own in its aftermath distinctly recall the pre-apocalyptic situation that Western societies experienced in the 1930s. Worrying trends in our current predicament are, first, a popular dissatisfaction with political elites and despondency in the face of the seemingly inexorable ascendance of the populist right in many countries; second, an alarming surge in economic inequality, with the withering of the middle class and the emergence of a vast underclass of working poor; and third, a widening chasm between intellectual elites and the proverbial ordinary people so that the former tend to preach only in an echo chamber, leading to the decline of empathy in the public sphere. The Covid crisis has laid bare the complex interplay between power, knowledge, and public health governance, with intellectuals occupying a crucial yet contentious position throughout. It has underscored their responsibility in failing to uphold democratic values, promote transparency, and engage in rigorous debate.

Worse, Carlo Caduff has noted that the power to respond to the Covid crisis has dazzled the intellectual elites in a complex and perverse combination:

> Pandemic fear is unnerving and mentally exhausting. Yet for those who embrace the feeling, it has the power of sustaining a state of excitement—excitement derived from the secret

> pleasure of spoiling a precious thing, wasting enormous resources, and engaging in an all-consuming project with total dedication. What we might call the provocation of the crisis—its intensification, expansion, and totalization beyond any notion of utility—seems so excessive and extreme that it borders on sheer madness. What could be more dangerous, more daring, more exciting than a walk on the wild side, an excursion to the other side of reason?[1]

Public health experts had been preparing for a major influenza pandemic for years, and Covid presented an ideal opportunity to unleash this energy.[2] And as an authoritarian temptation has been historically recurrent on the left, it now found a new pretext to be mobilized.[3] Let us deconstruct what happened here.

The origins of wokeness and critical theory

The roots of popular dissatisfaction with elites, economic inequality, and the estrangement of intellectuals from ordinary people can be traced back to the onset of globalization, a transformative economic model that gained prominence during the era of Margaret Thatcher and Ronald Reagan in the 1980s. Globalization fueled aspirations for improved living standards and unrestricted consumption, a trend that played a significant role also in the collapse of the Berlin Wall as people behind the Iron Curtain sought to partake in the growing Western prosperity.

---

1 Caduff, "What Went Wrong."

2 See Carlo Caduff, *The Pandemic Perhaps: Dramatic Events in a Public Culture of Danger* (Oakland, CA: University of California Press, 2015). See also Bonilla, "Covid, Twitter, and Critique."

3 See this volume with an eloquent title: Elena Lange, Geoff Shullenberger, eds., *Covid-19 and the Left: The Tyranny of Fear* (London: Routledge, 2024).

Liberal intellectuals as a social class endured a seismic upheaval with the fall of communism in 1989, even in Western Europe. To defend a vision of social engineering reminiscent of Mitterrand's first mandate as French president (1981-1988), for instance, suddenly became inconceivable. The left relinquished its pursuit of economic equality, while the working class fervently embraced mass consumption, both in the East *and* the West. For the left to enjoy wealth became permissible and even desirable in the 1990s, while the notion of the public good suffered a palpable blow. Tony Blair and Gerhard Schröder personified a new shamelessness among Western liberal political elites in which individuals sought political office not as a noble calling but as a means to amass personal fortunes after the end of their mandate. More recently, entrepreneurs such as Donald Trump, Rishi Sunak, and the Czech leader Andrej Babiš achieved billionaire status before they even entered the political arena, ostensibly with benevolent intentions but in large part to consolidate or expand their wealth thanks to their elected mandate.

Faced with the ideological crisis of the left and the growing division of society, liberal intellectuals found a new cause to champion: identity politics. Critical theory had questioned strategies of domination and the way they had been made invisible; identity politics now essentialized these strategies, regardless of whether intellectuals were now going against the principles of critical theory.[4] After all, what better topic to reflect upon than their own existential crisis? They heralded anti-racism, sexual minorities, feminism, and the defense of minorities. Predictably, the more the progressive and liberal left distanced itself from the toiling masses, the more radical it became.

4 Many thanks to Éloïse Adde for her input here.

Wokeness as a social practice of domination

This phenomenon is not without recalling the 1930s either. George Orwell savagely castigated the intelligentsia of his days as "every fruit-juice drinker, nudist, sandal-wearer, sex-maniac, Quaker, 'Nature Cure' quack, pacifist, and feminist in England." Only such an educated person, he mused, could be so distant from the "genuine proletarian."[5]

George Orwell harbored no desire to destroy the left; on the contrary, he embraced socialism, the kind of democratic socialism that championed social justice and common decency over power and privilege. He endured homelessness in London and the life of a miserable dishwasher in Paris, where he experienced hunger and faced near-death in a dilapidated hospital. He descended into a Welsh coal shaft and shared the life of miners to capture their everyday struggle. He fought in the Spanish Civil War, where he took a bullet in the throat and nearly died, then was hunted by Stalinist henchmen who would rather kill fellow left-wing activists than tolerate potential dissenters. Orwell and his wife narrowly evaded their clutches, an experience which provided the basis for his deconstruction of the Stalinist dictatorship in *Animal Farm* and *Nineteen Eighty-Four*. During one or another of these adventures, he contracted the tuberculosis from which he died at the premature age of 46.

How would a no-nonsense democratic socialist as Orwell have interpreted the reaction to Covid? As the pandemic unfolded in the Western world, despite local nuances in timelines and varying levels of cynicism, the virus modeled a society that he would have doubtless vehemently opposed. The left abandoned its commitment to defend the disadvantaged,

5 George Orwell, *The Road to Wigan Pier* (London: Gollancz, 1936), chapter 11, available here: https://www.george-orwell.org/The_Road_to_Wigan_Pier/10.html.

especially children, during the pandemic, opting instead for (self-)sycophancy; the national debt of many countries developed at an alarming pace, reaching levels not witnessed since the eve of the 1789 Revolution in France, for instance,[6] due to the fact that the wealthy are now undertaxed;[7] and crucial personalities within the political class in many Western countries have prioritized individual wealth accumulation over the public good.

Orwell would have recognized another familiar trope, too: an authoritarian fetishism within the intellectual left, which reappears time and again in history in the name of a brighter future that requires momentary sacrifices. This time around, it is wokeness. Herbert Marcuse, sometimes considered the "father of wokeness," wrote a famous essay in 1965 entitled "Repressive Tolerance."[8] Can tolerance be repressive? This is the whole question, one to which George Orwell or Karl Popper would certainly say no. There is a strong temptation within the current left to abandon democracy as an ideal, especially after being proven so wrong with Covid. In 2024, the famous *Guardian* columnist, icon of the liberal left and fervent supporter of a repressive version of the Covid response, George Monbiot, penned an editorial claiming that elections are a "travesty of democracy" and "people" must find a "real voice" in order to have "real representation." He claimed: "An

---

6 See Simon Brunfaut, "Thomas Piketty, économiste: 'Nous sommes dans une situation très proche de celle de la Révolution française,'" *L'écho*, September 11, 2021, https://www.lecho.be/opinions/general/thomas-piketty-economiste-nous-sommes-dans-une-situation-tres-proche-de-celle-de-la-revolution-francaise/10331365.html.

7 Emmie Martin, "Warren Buffet and Bill Gates Agree That the Rich Should Pay Higher Taxes—Here's What They Suggest," *CNBC*, February 26, 2019, https://www.cnbc.com/2019/02/25/warren-buffett-and-bill-gates-the-rich-should-pay-higher-taxes.html.

8 The full text is available here: https://www.marcuse.org/herbert/publications/1960s/1965-repressive-tolerance-fulltext.html.

election is a device for maximizing conflict and minimizing democracy." A better system might be, according to him, a "lottery vote."[9] The *New York Times* also sees the American constitution as "a threat for democracy"[10] or as "obstructing democracy,"[11] while the First Amendment guaranteeing free speech allegedly is "out of control."[12]

Monbiot shows that it is easier to call for the end of democracy than to apologize for supporting our undemocratic response to Covid, a demonstration if ever that to dehumanize a group of the population delegitimizes its authors.

From compliance to enforcement: The irresistible temptation of authority

The liberal left, which has largely sought refuge in the past decades in the field of education and quality mainstream media, flocked with Covid "towards the smell of 'progress' like bluebottles to a dead cat"[13] (another Orwell metaphor), with the caveat that modern-day intellectual "heroes" forsake the opportunity to take a bullet in the throat to safeguard democracy; instead, they stay home to save lives and wear a mask

9 George Monbiot, "General Elections Are a Travesty of Democracy—Let's Give the People a Real Voice," *The Guardian*, June 6, 2024, https://www.theguardian.com/commentisfree/article/2024/jun/06/general-elections-democracy-lottery-representation.

10 Jennifer Szalai, "The Constitution Is Sacred: Is It Also Dangerous? One of the Biggest Threats to America's Politics Might Be the Country's Founding Document," *The New York Times*, August 31, 2024, https://www.nytimes.com/2024/08/31/books/review/constitution-secession-democracy-crisis.html.

11 Letters to the editor, "Is the Constitution Obstructing American Democracy?" *The New York Times*, August 29, 2022, https://www.nytimes.com/2022/08/29/opinion/letters/constitution-democracy.html.

12 Tim Wu, "The First Amendment Is out of Control," *The New York Times*, July 2, 2024, https://www.nytimes.com/2024/07/02/opinion/supreme-court-net-choice-free-speech.html.

13 Orwell, *The Road to Wigan Pier*.

to protect you. Behind this virtuous façade lies, of course, a sanctimonious exploitation of delivery workers. Working-class laborers remained at liberty to die from Covid so long as they posed no risk of contamination to liberals. Irony lied in the meticulous disinfection of home-delivered goods coupled with impassioned lectures on moral virtue, all delivered through the conduit of mostly cozy homes and powerful Wi-Fi connections and computer equipment, of which the disadvantaged had only a downgraded version, if at all.

Today, the mainstream media fail to remind their audience that the considerable inflation we are experiencing is coming from being paid to stay at home and do little or nothing for months on end while our governments printed money.[14] Determined not to question the policy of lockdown, they blame the cost-of-living crisis on the Russia-Ukraine and Hamas-Israeli wars and conveniently forget that the inflation started long before these aggravating factors.[15]

One of the most irksome paradoxes of the Covid response is that academics who righteously stand against the rise of inequalities in normal circumstances supported a Covid response which dramatically increased inequalities. The disadvantaged were free to plunge into ever greater poverty in exchange for a fleeting sense of security for the intellectuals, while the world's billionaires found themselves

14 Éric Desrosiers, "Qui règlera l'addition de la crise de la Covid-19, selon Thomas Piketty?" *Le Devoir*, November 17, 2020, https://www.ledevoir.com/economie/589869/coronavirus-qui-reglera-l-addition.

15 Phillip Imman, "Leading Economies Sliding into Recession as Ukraine War Cuts Growth, OECD finds," *The Guardian*, September 26, 2022, https://www.theguardian.com/business/2022/sep/26/leading-economies-sliding-into-recession-as-ukraine-war-cuts-growth-finds-oecd. See also Richard Partington, "Escalating Middle East Conflict Could Send Global Inflation Soaring, Says S&P," *The Guardian*, October 28, 2023, https://www.theguardian.com/business/2023/oct/18/escalating-middle-east-conflict-could-send-global-inflation-soaring-says-rp.

US $4 trillion richer by the end of the first year of the pandemic.[16] Meanwhile, any form of criticism became "fake news." Alan Sokal remarked in a piece evocatively entitled "Free Speech and Fashionable Hypocrisy" that academic freedom is defended only when it buttresses "politically correct" narratives.[17] Intellectuals found themselves as incapable of challenging intellectual conformity and obedience as they were of defending free speech.[18]

While studying the Stalinist period in Czechoslovakia, I had always wondered how Czech intellectuals could be so blind as to loudly support the implausible propaganda promoted by Stalinist leaders while suppressing their own critical doubts—a conundrum which they collectively reflected upon and apologized for during the 1968 Prague Spring and its aftermath, becoming once again the charming intellectuals they had doubtless been before Stalinism. In the 1970s and 1980s, they often became respected dissidents, too.

The Covid pandemic has illustrated anew the tendency of intellectuals to fall prey to ideology and purported good intentions while momentarily endorsing dehumanization. Perhaps an apology is still coming, like in Czechoslovakia, where it took sixteen years from the most egregious Stalinist show trial in 1952 to the 1968 Prague Spring. In the US and on the other side of the political spectrum, it took eight years for the similarly dogmatic McCarthyism to be completely overcome and discarded. On the other hand, it took 90 years for the *New York Times* to present an apology of sorts to its readers for the lies of its star reporter, Moscow correspondent

---

16 Green, "Covid-19 and the Left."

17 Alan Sokal, "Free Speech and Fashionable Hypocrisy," *The Critic*, January 24, 2024, https://thecritic.co.uk/free-speech-and-fashionable-hypocrisy/.

18 Steve Salaita, "The Customs of Obedience in Academe," *No Flags, No Slogans* (blog), February 12, 2024, https://stevesalaita.com/the-customs-of-obedience-in-academe/.

Walter Duranty.[19] Duranty was granted the 1932 Pulitzer Prize for his glowing reports of Stalin's collectivization, even though it resulted in a famine that killed millions in Ukraine, the Holodomor, now considered a full-fledged genocide. He also vilified other reporters for allegedly twisting the truth.[20] Covid really has brought nothing new.

A new form of illiberalism is also revealing itself in other themes than Covid. In 2020, James Bennet, editor of the Opinion section at the *New York Times*, published an op-ed by Tom Cotton, Republican Senator of Arkansas, which went counter to the opinion of many of Bennet's colleagues and of the readers of the *New York Times*: in the context of the George Floyd scandal, Cotton called for the deployment of federal troops in American cities in case of violent rioting. The scandal was such, even though it was only an op-ed which did not implicate the editorial line of the paper, that Bennet resigned. Three years later, he went over this episode in a piece for the *Economist*, referring to the insufficient support of *NYT* publisher A.G. Sulzberger:

> The *Times*'s problem has metastasized from liberal bias to illiberal bias, from an inclination to favor one side of the national debate to an impulse to shut debate down altogether. All the empathy and humility in the world will not mean much against the pressures of intolerance and tribalism without an invaluable quality that Sulzberger did not emphasize: courage.[21]

19 See "New York Times Statement about 1932 Pulitzer Prize Awarded to Walter Duranty," undated, https://www.nytco.com/company/prizes-awards/new-york-times-statement-about-1932-pulitzer-prize-awarded-to-walter-duranty/. See also David Folkenflik, "'The New York Times Can't Shake the Cloud over a 90-Year-Old Pulitzer Prize," *NPR*, May 8, 2022, https://www.npr.org/2022/05/08/1097097620/new-york-times-pulitzer-ukraine-walter-duranty.

20 Gareth Jones, for instance. See the film *Mr. Jones* by Agnieszka Holland (2019), https://www.imdb.com/title/tt6828390/.

21 James Bennet, "When the New York Times Lost Its Way," *The Economist*,

Intolerance, tribalism, and cowardice were further compounded by authoritarianism and inhumanity during Covid. This is where George Orwell, again, is right on point. He keenly observed that progressivism is generally not driven by a genuine desire to combat misery or champion freedom but is rather rooted in a "hypertrophied sense of order." He noted that "to many people calling themselves Socialists, revolution does not mean a movement of the masses with which they hope to associate themselves; it means a set of reforms which 'we,' the clever ones, are going to impose upon 'them,' the Lower Orders."[22] During Covid, inhumanity became widespread even among scholars of the humanities.[23] The "proper left," derides French comedian Régis Mailhot, is now the left "which smells good from the armpits."[24]

The ease with which critical thinking was discarded while many intellectuals didn't harbor any doubt about their own infallibility is truly disconcerting. Edward Skidelsky speaks of a "slow erosion of moral and intellectual standards of which commercialism and wokery are merely the effect": "Many are convinced that 'freedom of thought' must conceal a toxic right-wing agenda—as if the left had no possible interest in intellectual freedom."[25]

December 14, 2023, https://www.economist.com/1843/2023/12/14/when-the-new-york-times-lost-its-way.

22 Orwell, *The Road to Wigan Pier*.

23 See this article: Michael Hiltzik, "Mocking Anti-Vaxxers' COVID Deaths Is Ghoulish, Yes—but May Be Necessary," *Los Angeles Times*, January 10, 2022, https://www.latimes.com/business/story/2022-01-10/why-shouldnt-we-dance-on-the-graves-of-anti-vaxxers.

24 "Régis Mailhot: pour Stéphane Bern, 'on va tous bouffer du Fillon pendant cinq ans,'" À la bonne heure (radio talk show), *RTL*, November 22, 2017, https://www.youtube.com/watch?v=2F45-xEclmU.

25 Edward Skidelsky, "It's Time to Stop the Rot: Students Denounced, Lecturers Cowed and Managers with Little Interest in Truth," *The Critic*, March 2024, https://thecritic.co.uk/issues/march-2024/its-time-to-stop-the-rot/.

A democratic society does not sacrifice ethics with impunity

The attitude of liberal intellectuals has proved not only counterproductive in the fight against Covid but dangerous as well. With the passing years and the subsiding panic, the staggering level of corruption and/or conflict of interest around the vaccine is slowly being revealed—one of the most egregious examples being, if I may repeat myself, that the NIH is a co-owner of the vaccine patent and has stood to make $1.2 billion and counting from its "objective" vaccine recommendation to the public.[26] The so-called "Pfizergate" involving EU President Ursula von der Leyen, coined the "scandal of the century" by journalist Thomas Fazi, also deserves thorough investigation, one which is however slow in coming. In the name of the EU, von der Leyen single-handedly signed off on a $35 billion deal with Pfizer, i.e., fifteen times the cost of production per dose of vaccine, mainly by text messages and phone calls, texts which she has still refused to hand over upon the completion of this manuscript in September 2024.[27]

Still, liberal intellectuals and political elites don't collectively appear to be anywhere near conceding that they made a grave mistake in relinquishing their critical ability during the pandemic. Only a few individuals have displayed the courage and honesty to do so.[28] Intellectuals who supported censorship

---

26 Alexander Tin, "Moderna Offers NIH Co-Ownership of COVID Vaccine Patent amid Dispute with Government," *CBC News*, November 15, 2021, https://www.cbsnews.com/news/moderna-covid-vaccine-patent-dispute-national-institutes-health/.

27 Thomas Fazi, "Von der Leyen Could Still Be Toppled," *UnHerd*, May 31, 2024, https://unherd.com/2024/05/pfizergate-could-still-topple-von-der-leyen/.

28 See Danny Kruger, "We MPs Need to Recognize That What We Did to the Country during Covid Was Wrong," *The Daily Sceptic*, January 30, 2024, https://dailysceptic.org/2024/01/30/we-mps-need-to-recognise-that-what-we-did-to-the-country-during-covid-was-wrong/. See also Larry Elliot, "The Price Britain Paid for Lockdown Was Colossal. Was There an Alternative?" *The*

then would rather continue supporting censorship now than admit they were wrong.

Disparaging democracy is worrisome because it paves the way for ever more authoritarian measures. Compounded by a media landscape that no longer scrutinizes power but rather defends it, our civic societies find themselves defenseless. Traditional media appear rather unfazed by the censorship imposed by various states on social media, perhaps because, as already mentioned, social media had effectively put an end to their privileged position as political commentator in the public sphere, and they are thus getting rid of a powerful competitor. In this precarious state, the need for figures of the George Orwell format becomes increasingly urgent—individuals unyielding to power and committed to portraying the unvarnished truth, irrespective of its potential to unsettle those in authority. Will we find enough of them, and will we find them in time?

To externalize criticism of the lockdown to the extreme right was an egregious mistake

Before Covid, critical approaches to censorship and the surveillance state were traditionally viewed as left-wing and progressive. However, when surveillance and the biosecurity state gained unexpected actuality during the Covid crisis, critics were swiftly labeled right-wing or even alt-right—

Guardian, February 12, 2023, https://www.theguardian.com/business/2023/feb/12/price-britain-paid-lockdown-colossal-alternative-recession-austerity-stagnation; Bennet, "When the New York Times Lost Its Way"; and Nadeen Badshah, "Matt Hancock Wanted to 'Frighten Everyone' into Following Covid Rules,'" *The Guardian*, March 5, 2023, https://www.theguardian.com/politics/2023/mar/05/matt-hancock-wanted-to-frighten-everyone-into-following-covid-rules.

including not only Agamben, as seen above, but also Glenn Greenwald, who had been one of the *Guardian* journalists who had been awarded the Pulitzer Prize in 2014 for his investigation of global surveillance programs on the basis of Edward Snowden's revelations.

The pernicious aspect of the Covid censorship is that it has ensnared the liberal left in a trap. It has proven impossible to enforce censorship and defend democracy at the same time—the "miracle" has not happened.[29] Legitimizing censorship to defend public health amounted to playing with fire, even when, or if, the public approved.[30] Barbara Stiegler points out that to oppose health and freedom was a "fallacious narrative." She underlines that the measures taken in France against the virus weakened not only the most vulnerable but also the very concept of public health. When health is opposed to freedom, patients' rights give way to an "authoritarian, centralized, and neoliberal health policy."[31]

To relinquish the defense of freedom to the extreme right is one of the most egregious political missteps of the Covid response, one that might cost several Western democracies dearly. By labeling anyone advocating fundamental freedoms

29 I borrow the term "miracle" from Abdennour Bidar, *Démocratie en danger: Dix questions sur la crise sanitaire et ses conséquences* (Paris: Les liens qui libèrent, 2022), 19.

30 More than half of the American public now apparently thinks the First Amendment guaranteeing free speech goes "too far," although it is now hard to tell, because of censorship, if it is public opinion which pushed liberal intellectuals to criticize free speech or vice versa. See Laurel Duggan, "Majority of Americans Think First Amendment Goes Too Far," *UnHerd*, August 1, 2024, https://unherd.com/newsroom/majority-of-americans-think-first-amendment-goes-too-far/.

31 "Barbara Stiegler, santé publique et libertés," *France Culture*, May 17, 2022, https://www.radiofrance.fr/franceculture/podcasts/tracts-le-podcast/barbara-stiegler-sante-publique-et-libertes-1994435. See also her two essays: Barbara Stiegler, *De la démocratie en pandémie*, and Barbara Stiegler and François Alla, *Santé publique année zéro* (Paris: Gallimard, 2022).

"extreme right," our societies have inadvertently granted to the extreme right the agency and legitimacy to represent anyone who still thinks freedom is a value worth fighting for. To defend liberty has become the new subversive attitude, one which is bound to seduce the voters.

Why the liberal left has chosen to embark on this self-destructive path is perplexing, all the more so that once in power, the extreme right is likely to put an end to its sudden commitment to "freedom" and to dismantle what remained of the liberal movement. Pierre Gentillet is a jurist and ideologue of the French extreme right movement Rassemblement National (National Rally), which captured 37% of the votes in the July 7, 2024, French parliamentary elections. The lesson he draws from the Covid response is unequivocal and chilling:

> I'm optimistic because the rule of law is dying.... We have observed under Covid that when a politician decrees an emergency situation (I remind you that Covid was not all that urgent in proportion to the measures we took), the rule of law can be overcome. During this political crisis, politics really took precedence over the law. So, this is why I'm optimistic: if, tomorrow, we want to emancipate ourselves from certain treaties—not just the European Union treaty, but other treaties as well—from certain standards that are poisoning us, well, provided we bring the Constitutional Court into line, we will be able to do anything we want. Politics is now back at the top of the hierarchy of concrete standards.[32]

How to bring the Constitutional Court "into line"? Pierre Gentillet proposed two "solutions": either by dismantling it entirely since he no longer sees it as necessary for the functioning

32 Chaîne officielle TVL, "L'Etat de droit se meurt, le Peuple retrouve enfin le pouvoir—Le Zoom—Pierre Gentillet—TVL," YouTube video, 24:17, April 8, 2022, https://www.youtube.com/watch?v=JaijKWPAcTc&t=710s.

of the state, or by appointing new justices to the court in the name of a better representation of the "real people" until the old, presumably hostile, justices are in the minority.[33]

Human rights lawyer Patrice Spinosi deems this prospective tactic "extremely worrying."[34] He deconstructed in 2024 how "emergency measures" and "legal exemptions" are almost always instrumentalized, and the threat justifying these measures tends to "never disappear." Nevertheless, in the case of Covid he inexplicably had no objection to the emergency measures. Four years later, he still deemed them necessary and unavoidable. That "we didn't know" and the measures were "only transitory" compounded in his view the deprivation of public freedoms they entailed.

And yet, thanks to the Covid response, "momentary" restrictions such as QR codes to prevent people from freely moving around and censorship on social media to prevent "dangerous behaviors" became part and parcel of our societies. The adoption of such measures was made possible only thanks to an artificial "scientific consensus" itself predicated on silencing dissident voices. We *did* know that the Covid measures were disproportionate to the threat, or even more to the point, we could and would have known if the debate hadn't been stifled. A censorship practice which was implemented for a would-be "just cause" and "only for a short while" significantly weakened the rule of law long after the emergency had passed, and it created a dangerous precedent.

Censorship was and remains unacceptable in a democracy, especially during a crisis when collective intelligence

---

33 Chaîne officielle, "L'État de droit se meurt."

34 See the radio talk show hosted by Charles Pépin, "Patrice Spinosi: comment défendre les libertés publiques?" "Sous le soleil de Platon," *France Inter*, July 11, 2024, https://www.radiofrance.fr/franceinter/podcasts/sous-le-soleil-de-platon/sous-le-soleil-de-platon-du-jeudi-11-juillet-2024-1076019.

must be crucially mobilized. Without censorship, alternative policies could have been discussed since the beginning, and many lives might have been saved. If or when these censorship tools fall into even worse hands, as appears almost inevitable considering the economic crisis and popular discontent unleashed by the lockdowns (18 countries of the EU out of 27 are in danger of falling into the hands of the extreme right), the consequences for democracy are potentially devastating.

Postscript

When I submitted my manuscript for peer review in May 2024, I concluded with a warning: the catastrophic mishandling of the Covid response and the refusal of the establishment to acknowledge, let alone address, their own failures could pave the way for the extreme right in several countries. Since then, far-right parties have won or made significant electoral gains in France, Hungary, Italy, Austria, Slovakia, the eastern provinces of Germany, the Netherlands, and Romania, while Donald Trump won the US election.

The liberal left has yet to reckon with the consequences of its contempt for the lower half of society. Mainstream media narratives and social media feeds have attributed Donald Trump's reelection to racism, sexism, and the stupidity of the American electorate, while they studiously avoid contemplating their own responsibility in the Democrats' debacle. A few American colleagues have openly resorted to labeling students they suspect of supporting Donald Trump as "fascists."

The journal *Scientific American* exemplifies the politicization of science and the erosion of professional boundaries that have become characteristic of the Covid era. On election night, its editor-in-chief, Laura Helmuth, posted on Bluesky: "Solidarity to everybody whose meanest, dumbest, most bigoted high-school classmates are celebrating early results because fuck them to the moon and back. I apologize to younger voters that my Gen X is so full of fucking fascists."[35]

35 Maya Yang, "Scientific American Editor Steps down after Calling Trump Supporters 'Fascists' and 'Bigoted'," *The Guardian*, November 16, 2024, https://www.theguardian.com/media/2024/nov/16/scientific-american-editor-steps-down.

She resigned after the backlash her remarks generated, yet her statement encapsulates the left's tendency to blame voters for failing to meet its expectations, rather than the other way around. This attitude has left many progressives struggling to comprehend why segments of the Democrats' traditional base—including many Latinos and African Americans—opted to vote for Donald Trump over a Black woman.[36]

Such a reaction reminds me of Bertolt Brecht's famous quip in "The Solution," written in 1953 after the East German Communist Party blamed the people for rebelling against their rule: "Some party hack decreed that the people had lost the government's confidence and could only regain it with redoubled effort. If that is the case, would it not be simpler if the government simply dissolved the people and elected another?"[37] As with communism studies, we would do well to adopt a social perspective on Covid rather than a political one. It would allow us to understand the present developments through the lived experiences of individuals and communities, rather than be constrained by political dogma and ideological frameworks.

While Bernie Sanders and Chris Cuomo have made commendable efforts to confront the Democrats' "betrayal of the working class" and their "mass delusion,"[38] "limousine liberals"

---

36 John Harris, "From Trump's Victory, a Simple, Inescapable Message: Many People Despise the Left," *The Guardian*, November 10, 2024, https://www.theguardian.com/commentisfree/2024/nov/10/donald-trump-the-left-social-media-rightwing-propaganda-progressives-woke.

37 See the entry "Die Lösung," *Wikipedia*, https://en.wikipedia.org/wiki/Die_Lösung.

38 See Bernie Sanders' Twitter post (@BernieSanders), "It should come as no great surprise that a Democratic Party which has abandoned working class people would find that the working class has abandoned them," Twitter, November 6, 2024, 10:14 pm, https://x.com/BernieSanders/status/1854271157135941698, and Chris Cuomo's (@ChrisCuomo), "So, we learned last night a political truth," Twitter, November 7, 2024, 2:59 am, https://x.com/ChrisCuomo/status/1854342764722364569.

remain far from questioning whether their "sneering condescension" and "exclusion" of ordinary voters has been a productive strategy.[39] Instead, they appear intent on already preparing their defeat in 2028. Comedian Bill Maher, known for his left-leaning sympathies but also for being an unabashed critic, remarked how amazing it was that an electoral disaster of such magnitude "still doesn't put a dent in the thinking that lost it."[40] On his HBO show *Real Time*, Maher added:

> The reason I'm so mad at the Democrats is because as a voter, the issues that were important to me were democracy and the environment. And now there's no one to champion or defend either of them because you, with your aggressively anti-common sense agenda and shitty exclusionary attitude, blew it. You lost everything, the House, Senate, White House, Supreme Court, and left us completely unprotected and ready to be violated.[41]

One word that Democrats and liberals worldwide have rarely uttered in the wake of their electoral defeats is "lockdown." Their indignation has failed to spark reflection on the lockdown policies that proved to be economic insanity for a working class whose livelihood depended on going out to work. The inflation caused by months of paying people to stay

---

39 I borrow these expressions from Bridget Phetasy, "Lectures from Limousine Liberals," *Tablet*, October 19, 2022, https://www.tabletmag.com/sections/news/articles/lectures-from-limousine-liberals.

40 See Bill Maher's Twitter post (@billmaher), "It's amazing how an election loss, even as big as this one, still doesn't put a dent in the thinking that lost it," Twitter, November 16, 2024, 5:03 am, https://x.com/billmaher/status/1857635615031934984.

41 Zachary Leeman, "Bill Maher Goes Scorched Earth on Dems for 'Doubling Down' on 'Anti-Common Sense Agenda' after Losses: 'Stop Digging!'" *Mediaite*, November 16, 2024, https://www.mediaite.com/tv/bill-maher-goes-scorched-earth-on-dems-for-doubling-down-on-anti-common-sense-agenda-after-losses-stop-digging/.

home pushed the middle class toward financial instability and drove many in the lower middle class into outright poverty. Economic inequality has reached new levels in both the West and the developing world, reversing decades of progress.[42] While liberal media outlets find moral gratification in criticizing figures like Elon Musk for "spreading disinformation," and while they make a show of abandoning Twitter for Bluesky, they seldom reflect on how pandemic-era economic policies dramatically increased Musk's fortune and influence. As for the idea that a less invasive approach, such as focused protection, might have been a better response to Covid, it remains anathema.

Such moral posturing has hindered liberals from addressing the deep-seated corruption surrounding the pharmaceutical industry in the Covid vaccine rollout. One glaring example is the conflict of interest involving Anthony Fauci, who led a public institution that co-owned the patent for the Covid vaccine while ostensibly offering impartial guidance to the public. This concerning overlap remains either ignored or suppressed by mainstream media. Moreover, the combined forces of censorship and self-censorship—arguably the most extensive since World War II—are still partially intact. Kamala Harris, during her campaign, even pledged to reinforce censorship. For those not swept up in self-righteous narratives, the so-called "mystery" behind Trump's appeal becomes less perplexing.

While Trump's campaign promises are unreliable, the Covid narrative has been rapidly unraveling in the fall of 2024. One of the president-elect's most discussed prospective cabinet appointments is Robert F. Kennedy Jr. as Secretary of

42 See Kevin Bardosh, "How Did the COVID Pandemic Response Harm Society? A Global Evaluation and State of Knowledge Review (2020-21)," *SSRN*, May 24, 2023, https://papers.ssrn.com/sol3/papers.cfm?abstract_id=4447806.

Health and Human Services (HHS). This department wields significant influence, overseeing key health agencies that were central during the Covid crisis, such as the Food and Drug Administration (FDA), the National Institutes of Health (NIH), and its division—the National Institute of Allergy and Infectious Diseases (NIAID). The possibility of Kennedy taking charge of HHS has sparked outrage in liberal circles. Yet, his commitment to confront the entrenched power and influence of Big Pharma is difficult to dispute.[43]

Two recent documentaries involving figures of the Covid dissent movement have critically examined the pharmaceutical industry and its profound influence on healthcare. Aseem Malhotra's *First! Do No Pharm*, released in September 2024, sheds light on how Western healthcare systems have been commandeered by profit-driven pharmaceutical corporations.[44] The film delves into controversies surrounding statin-type drugs, Vioxx, Zoloft, and Ozempic. It also highlights the immense pressure exerted on physicians who challenge the status quo, including Malhotra himself: he publicly questioned the safety of mRNA vaccines after his father suffered a fatal heart attack following a Covid vaccine booster and he was shunned for it.[45] The documentary, however, also showcases figures of integrity, such as Fiona Godlee, the former editor-in-chief of the *British Medical Journal*. Godlee's decision to publish and defend Paul D. Thacker's article critiquing Pfizer's Covid vaccine trials in 2021 that I discussed in

43 Jay Bhattacharya and Kevin Bardosh, "RFK Jr Will Disrupt the US Medical Establishment," *UnHerd*, November 15, 2024, https://unherd.com/newsroom/rfk-jr-will-disrupt-the-us-medical-establishment/.

44 See https://www.imdb.com/title/tt33511587/.

45 Frank Chung, "British Cardiologist Calls for mRNA Vaccines to Be Suspended Due to Heart Risks," *News.com.au*, June 9, 2023, https://www.news.com.au/lifestyle/health/health-problems/british-cardiologist-calls-for-mrna-vaccines-to-be-suspended-due-to-heart-risks/news-story/7ced98559a790d325afc44ceb9cc2b95.

Chapter 2 was a rare act of courage in a field dominated by corporate influence.[46]

A second noteworthy documentary, Jenner Furst's ironically titled *Thank You, Dr. Fauci*, premiered in November 2024.[47] One of its most striking revelations comes from Robert Redfield, head of the Centers for Disease Control and Prevention (CDC) as the Covid outbreak unfolded. Redfield now openly supports the lab leak hypothesis, stating, "My own view is that this virus was not of natural origin; it was an act of scientific arrogance."[48] Also this film scrutinizes a number of missteps by the pharmaceutical industry and the health agencies tasked with overseeing them. It highlights the troubling conflict of interest surrounding Peter Daszak, the president of EcoHealth Alliance, who directed research on high-risk viruses at the Wuhan Institute of Virology thanks to a grant approved by Anthony Fauci's NIAID.[49] In a startling case of cronyism, Daszak also led the 2021 World Health Organization delegation to Wuhan assigned to investigate the lab leak theory—unsurprisingly concluding that the virus was of zoonotic nature, not a lab leak, and thus exonerating himself and his organization.

Another significant figure featured in the film is Marty Makary, who also embraces the lab leak theory, describing it here as "the biggest industrial accident in the history of mankind." A vocal critic of Anthony Fauci,[50] Makary is also known

46 Thacker, "Covid-19: Researcher Blows the Whistle."

47 "Thank You, Dr. Fauci," https://www.imdb.com/title/tt34361382/.

48 See also Jess Thomson, "Trump's Former CDC Chief Suggests US Origin for COVID: 'Can't Prove That,'" *Newsweek*, November 19, 2024, https://www.newsweek.com/covid-19-lab-leak-theory-united-states-north-carolina-cdc-head-robert-redfield-trump-1987571.

49 See Sharon Lerner, Mara Hvistendahl, and Maia Hibbett, "NIH Documents Provide New Evidence U.S. Funded Gain-of-Function Research in Wuhan," *The Intercept*, September 9, 2021, https://theintercept.com/2021/09/09/covid-origins-gain-of-function-research/.

50 See Jay Bhattacharya and Bryce Nichols, "Conversations with Jay Bhattacharya:

for his no-nonsense positions against the pharmaceutical industry, detailed among others in his latest book, *Blind Spots*, a striking analysis of medical groupthink and arrogance.[51] What is relevant for us here is that he has been selected by the Trump administration as the next Commissioner of the Food and Drug Administration (FDA.)[52]

Even more consequential is the appointment of Jay Bhattacharya as director of the National Institutes of Health (NIH).[53] Bhattacharya, a scientist of polite and graceful manners who co-authored the Great Barrington Declaration and who has been a leading critic of the Biden administration's Covid response, has also gradually espoused the lab leak theory.[54] Prior to this potential nomination, he had actively refrained from taking any political stance. In fact, as mentioned above, he confessed to having opposed the consolidation of the censorship lawsuit of which he is a co-plaintiff, Murthy vs. Missouri, with the lawsuit led by Robert F. Kennedy Jr. vs. Biden. By being associated with RFK Jr., so to speak against their will, Aaron Kheriaty and Jay Bhattacharya discussed in August 2024 how they precisely feared the politicization of

---

Dr. Marty Makary (author, health care expert)," *Science from the Fringe* (podcast), November 4, 2024, https://sciencefromthefringe.substack.com/p/conversations-with-jay-bhattacharya-cc3.

51 Marty Makary, *Blind Spots: When Medicine Gets It Wrong, and What It Means for Our Health* (New York: Bloomsbury, 2024).

52 "Trump Nominates Marty Makary, Who Opposed COVID Vaccine Mandates, to Head FDA," *CBS News*, November 22, 2024, https://www.cbsnews.com/news/trump-marty-makary-fda-administrator/.

53 "Trump Picks Covid Lockdown Critic to Lead Top Health Agency," *BBC*, November 27, 2024, https://www.bbc.com/news/articles/cvg4yxmmg1zo.

54 See in particular Jay Bhattacharya, "How Did COVID-19 Originate? Ft Steven C. Quay," *The Illusion of Consensus* (podcast), October 5, 2024, https://www.illusionconsensus.com/p/how-did-covid-19-originate-ft-steven, as well as the fourth panel, "COVID-19 Origins and the Regulation of Virology," at the conference he convened at Stanford on October 4, 2024, "Pandemic Policy: Planning the Future, Assessing the Past," https://healthpolicy.fsi.stanford.edu/events/pandemic-policy-planning-future-assessing-past.

their case while the issue of censorship should remain apolitical in their view.[55] The irony is that Jay Bhattacharya and his friend Marty Makary found themselves, three months later, no doubt at the behest of the same RFK Jr., members of the Trump administration, where they will doubtless find it more challenging than ever to resist the politicization of science. While motivated by a noble aim, their mission is a gamble. Communist history does not bode well in this regard: individuals who tried to reform the system and serve the public good as insiders (in this case from within the communist party) lost credibility no matter their good intentions, while the dissidents who chose to retain their independence from politics eventually came out on top. We can only hope that, in this case, Bhattacharya's and Makary's integrity and vision of an apolitical science policy will prevail; time will tell if, to echo Dr. Fauci, it was a risk worth taking. Were they to succeed, it would be a momentous step forward in curbing the pharmaceutical corporate influence on the American state.

Finally, Republican Senator Rand Paul, a persistent critic of Fauci and of federal pandemic measures, is set to chair the Senate Homeland Security Committee as of January 2025. He has already vowed to focus on what he describes as "the Covid-19 coverup."[56]

Together, these appointments underscore a realignment in how the US may approach public health governance and accountability in the post-Covid era, unfortunately under

---

55 Jay Bhattacharya and Aaron Kheriaty, "The Worst Violation of Free Speech Rights in US History ft: Aaron Kheriaty," *The Illusion of Consensus* (podcast), August 6, 2024, https://www.illusionconsensus.com/p/new-the-worst-violation-of-free-speech.

56 Dan Diamond and Rachel Roubein, "Rand Paul Vows to Investigate 'Covid Coverup' as Senate Panel's New Chair," *The Washington Post*, November 14, 2024, https://www.washingtonpost.com/health/2024/11/14/rand-paul-covid-origins-senate-oversight-committee-chairman/.

Trump rather than Biden. They suggest that investigations into the pandemic's origins and policy decisions will remain a high-profile issue in the coming years. A significant reassessment might include a deeper investigation into the lab leak theory, into the potential risks associated with the Covid vaccine, and into Anthony Fauci's role in what can be seen, at the very least, as a minimization of both issues. The hypothesis that China's initial lockdown in Wuhan might have been less a response to the virus itself and more an effort to obscure a lab leak; the notion that Western countries might have been so dazzled by this dramatic overreaction that they sought to emulate it, while all it did was attempt to hide a blunder of historic proportion; the perspective that an American public health agency might have funded the research that caused the "biggest industrial accident in the history of mankind" while financially profiting from the vaccine that resulted from this research; and the prospect that Western liberals might have embraced censorship to avoid discussing their espousal of incompetence, authoritarianism, and corporate greed, are almost too painful to contemplate.

November 28, 2024

Bibliography

The Covid Librarian (a Twitter user) has compiled a useful list of volumes on the Covid response, including a category "Scholarly Topics" comprising humanities and social sciences: https://coroniverse.com/scholarly-topics-subdirectory/.

Agamben, Giorgio. *Where Are We Now? The Epidemic as Politics*. London: Eris, 2021.

Atlas, Scott. *A Plague upon Our House*. New York: Posthill Press, 2021.

Berenson, Alex. *Unreported Truths about Covid-19 and Lockdowns*. New York: Blue Deep, 2021.

Bidar, Abdennour. *Démocratie en danger: Dix questions sur la crise sanitaire et ses conséquences*. Paris: Les liens qui libèrent, 2022.

Briggs, Daniel, Anthony Ellis, Anthony Llyod, and Luke Telford. *Researching the Covid-19 Pandemic: A Critical Blueprint for the Social Sciences*. Bristol: Policy Press, 2021.

Briggs, Daniel, Luke Telford, Anthony Lloyd, Anthony Ellis, and Justin Kotzé. *Lockdown: Social Harm in the Covid-19 Era*. London: Palgrave Macmillan, 2021.

Briggs, Daniel, Luke Telford, Anthony Lloyd, and Anthony Ellis. *The New Futures of Exclusion: Life in the Covid-19 Aftermath*. London: Palgrave Macmillan, 2023.

Czarniawska, Barbara, Josef Pallas, and Elena Raviola, eds. *Covid-19 Stories from the Swedish Welfare State: The Pandemicracy*. Bristol: Bristol University Press, 2025.

Dodsworth Laura. *A State of Fear: How the UK Government Weaponized Fear during the Covid-19 Pandemic*. London: Pinter & Martin, 2021.

Girard, René, and Jean-Loup Bonnamy. *Quand la psychose fait dérailler le monde*. Paris: Gallimard–Tracts, 2020.

Green, Toby, and Thomas Fazi. *The Covid Consensus: The Global Assault on Democracy and the Poor—A Critique from the Left*. London: Hurst, 2023.

Hays II, George, Joshua M. Hayden, and Milada Polišenská, eds. *Leadership in the Time of Covid: Pandemic Responses in Central Europe.* Budapest–New York: CEU Press, 2023.

Kheriaty, Aaron. *The New Abnormal: The Rise of the Biomedical Security State.* Washington DC: Regnery, 2022.

Laignel-Lavastine, Alexandra. *La déraison sanitaire: Le Covid-19 et le culte de la vie par-dessus tout.* Paris: Le bord de l'eau, 2020.

Lange, Elena Louisa, and Geoff Shullenberger, eds. *Covid-19 and the Left: The Tyranny of Fear.* London: Routledge, 2024.

Maffesoli, Michel. *L'ère des soulèvements: Emeutes et confinements—Les derniers soubresauts de la modernité.* Paris: Le Cerf, 2021.

Makary, Marty. *Blind Spots: When Medicine Gets It Wrong, and What It Means for Our Health.* New York: Bloomsbury, 2024.

Mucchielli, Laurent. *La Doxa du Covid, Peur, santé, corruption et démocratie,* 2 vols. Bastia: Éoliennes, 2022.

Rouchier, Juliette, and Victorien Barbet. *La diffusion de la Covid-19: Que peuvent les modèles?* Paris: Matériologiques, 2020.

Stiegler, Barbara. *De la démocratie en pandémie: Santé, recherche, education.* Paris: Gallimard-Tracts, 2021.

Sutoris, Peter, Sinéad Murphy, Aleida Mendes Borges, and Yossi Nehushtan, eds. *Pandemic Response and the Cost of Lockdowns: Global Debates from Humanities and Social Sciences.* London: Routledge, 2023.

Index

Printed in the United States
by Baker & Taylor Publisher Services